THE BEST OF
BUSINESS CARD
DESIGN

{nine}

ROCKPORT

First published in the United States of America by Rockport Publishers, a member of Quayside Publishing Group

100 Cummings Center

Suite 406-L

Beverly, Massachusetts 01915-6101

Telephone: (978) 282-9590

Fax: (978) 283-2742

www.rockpub.com

ISBN-13: 978-1-59253-596-5

ISBN-10: 1-59253-596-8

10 9 8 7 6 5 4 3 2 1

Design: Rule29

Cover Image: Rule29

Printed in China

THE BEST OF
BUSINESS CARD
DESIGN

BEVERLY MASSACHUSETTS

{nine}

ROCKPORT PUBLISHERS

Research and cardomologist classifications by:

Rule29

CONTENTS

DESIGN RULE29   RULE29.COM

COVER IMAGE RULE29

INTRODUCTION

There are many theories on when and how *Cardious De Business* first evolved into its current state of being. This tome does not explore that question as much as it covers the various species and makeup of such an interesting hand-to-hand form of communication.

In an age of impersonal interaction, the rarity of fine examples of this elusive creature make it, as some might say, an endangered species. With great revelry we have scoured a global collection of samples that include some of the most *hottious designious* specimens seen in years.

Our experimental research may open your eyes to ideas that you may not have yet explored, ideas that may make you shout in agony by the sheer brilliance. Whatever your response, each of these specimens has a unique personality and makeup that in its environment creates a reaction, a conversation, or an impression.

We applaud those who participated in this adventure and hope that you enjoy this exhibit as much as we have delighted in curating it.

NOTES

TYPUS MAXIMUS

- BOLD & READABLE
- GREAT KERNING
- UNAFRAID OF DRAWING ATTENTION
- LARGE & IN CHARGE
- TYPE EXCLUSIVE

KEY CHARACTERISTICS

The following pages contain creatures with prominent typographical features that clearly set them apart from their more conservatively typeset brethren. These examples fall under the *Typus Maximus* genus and are commonly referred to as "big and beautiful." We believe that they formed these striking features in an attempt to quickly assert themselves at the top of the typographical food chain. The following is a rare collection of these highly readable and clearly unforgettable beauties.

NOTES

D*MNGOOD

OURS CREATIVE
DAVID MOUSSALLEM 214 ST. GEORGE STREET – 505 M5R 2
EMAIL OURSCREATIVE@GMAIL.COM TELEPHONE 1 905 616 2

craftman

RIO
ANEIRO
O LOURDES
3337 9116
WWW.THEART.COM.BR
THEART@THEART.COM.BR

ART
GRAND CENTER
LIFE ™

THE INTERSECTION OF
ART AND LIFE ™

ive
not decorative

for you

marc o'brien
visual communicator

marc@**marcobrien**.n
(804) 677–7655

am
pm

h   m

JOHN K.
FITZGERALD
LANDSCAPE DESIGN

VALLOTKARP

REEL BIOGRAPHY
38 WEST 39th ST · 2ND FLOOR
NEW YORK, NEW YORK 10018

TEL: 212-867-7287
FAX: 212-867-3756

REEL
BIOGRAPHY®

001

People Design

People Design

Hi, I'm **Adam Rice**. I'm a Graph
Design. Good work is fueled b
work is fueled by dark chocol
at adam@peopledesign.com

People Design helps people make g
people. We believe that good desig
makes things better. We work at 64
212, Grand Rapids, Michigan, 4950

peopledesign.com/adam

good design makes better thi
e work at 648 Monroe Avenue
chigan, 49503. Call us at 616 459

yang

evin Budelmann, designer and pla
t of People Design. I believe in the
of people solving problems for peo
eached at kevin@peopledesign.com

e Design helps people make good experiences
ple. We believe that good design makes better th
makes things better. We work at 648 Monroe Avenue
212, Grand Rapids, Michigan, 49503. Call us at 616 45

peopledesign.com/kevin

002

JOHN · K · FITZGERALD · **LANDSCAPE DESIGN**
514 · SOUTH · BEVERLY LANE
ARLINGTON HEIGHTS · ILLINOIS · 60005

WWW · JKFLANDSCAPE · COM

PHONE 847 · 722 · 4047 **FAX** 847 · 368 · 9823
EMAIL JOHN @ JKFLANDSCAPE · COM

003

«CREATING IS THE MOST FUN
YOU CAN HAVE WITH YOUR
CLOTHES ON.»
JERRY DELLA FEMINA

CARSTEN PRENGER
DIPLOM-DESIGNER
KÖNIGGRÄTZERSTRASSE 59
47053 DUISBURG
PHONE +49 (0)177.61.91.210
CARSTEN.PRENGER@GMX.NET

004

MSDS	*001*
DESIGN FIRM	SPECIMEN
Matthew Schwartz	
DESIGNER(S)	
Matthew Schwartz	
ART DIRECTOR	
Reel Biography	
CLIENT	
NOTES	
InDesign CS3	

People Design	*002*
DESIGN FIRM	SPECIMEN
Tim Calkins	
DESIGNER(S)	
Jonathan L. Smith	
ART DIRECTOR	
People Design	
CLIENT	

Real Art Design Group	*003*
DESIGN FIRM	SPECIMEN
Saundra Marcel	
DESIGNER(S)	
John K. Fitzgerald Landscape Design	
CLIENT	
NOTES	
Illustrator CS3; Starwhite Vicksburg, Tiara Smooth	

Carsten Prenger	*004*
DESIGN FIRM	SPECIMEN
Carsten Prenger	
ART DIRECTOR	
Carsten Prenger	
CLIENT	
NOTES	
InDesign CS3; Zanders Medley Pure	

Real Art Design Group	*001*
DESIGN FIRM	SPECIMEN

Saundra Marcel
DESIGNER(S)

Cater Brands, Inc.
CLIENT

NOTES
Illustrator CS3; Cougar Opaque

AFFINA	*002*
DESIGN FIRM	SPECIMEN

Jessica Zubrzycki
DESIGNER(S)

Renita Van Dusen
ART DIRECTOR

Ellen Shaffer
CLIENT

NOTES
Illustrator CS3; Letterpress

HI(NY), LLC	*003*
DESIGN FIRM	SPECIMEN

Hitomi Watanabe, Iku Oyamada
DESIGNER(S)

Hitomi Watanabe, Iku Oyamada
ART DIRECTOR

AS/D
CLIENT

NOTES
Illustrator CS3; Matte paper

CA+ER
brands

convenience is served.

kevin castle president

e kcastle@caterbrandsinc.com
5818 wilmington pike, suite 228
centerville, ohio 45459
p 937 848 6100   c 937 532 6960
f 937 848 6104
www.caterbrandsinc.com

001

eloquence is always effective

ellen shaffer

WRITER

e@ellenshaffer.com
651.222.1475 phone 651.222.1495 fax
165 western avenue north #308 saint paul, mn 55102

www.ellenshaffer.com

002

003

juan carlo bermudez
craftmanenterprise | president

2343 crescent street 1fl
astoria,ny 11105

917 612 4446

carlo@craftmannyc.com

AS/D ASOCIACIÓN DE DISEÑO
FERNANDO VELASCO RT
ARQUITECTO/DIRECTOR
FUENTE DE TEMPLANZA 33 TECAMACHALCO/EDO.MEX 53950
T 52 (55) 56 39 20 78
VELASCO@ASD-ARCHITECTURE.COM
WWW.ASD-ARCHITECTURE.COM

003

004

HI(NY), LLC	001
DESIGN FIRM	SPECIMEN
Hitomi Watanabe, Iku Oyamada	
DESIGNER(S)	
Hitomi Watanabe, Iku Oyamada	
ART DIRECTOR	
AS/D	
CLIENT	
NOTES	
Illustrator CS3, Photoshop CS3;	
Cougar Opaque 130 lb. Cover	

Hill Design Studios	002
DESIGN FIRM	SPECIMEN
Randy Hill	
DESIGNER(S)	
Randy Hill	
ART DIRECTOR	
Oregon Valley Boys	
CLIENT	
NOTES	
InDesign CS3; Neenah Classic Crest, Solar White 100 lb.	
Letterpressed metallic inks	

Grip Design	003
DESIGN FIRM	SPECIMEN
Josh Blaylock	
DESIGNER(S)	
Kelly Kaminski	
ART DIRECTOR	
Maxwell Aesthetics	
CLIENT	
NOTES	
Illustrator CS3	

Grip Design	004
DESIGN FIRM	SPECIMEN
Josh Blaylock	
DESIGNER(S)	
Kelly Kaminski	
ART DIRECTOR	
Goldberg Kohn	
CLIENT	
NOTES	
Illustrator CS3	

MSDS	001
DESIGN FIRM	SPECIMEN
Ryan Reynolds	
DESIGNER(S)	
Matthew Schwartz	
ART DIRECTOR	
Vallot Karp	
CLIENT	
NOTES	
CS3; Mohawk Navajo Brilliant White 130 lb.	

Steve Scott Graphic Design	002
DESIGN FIRM	SPECIMEN
Steve Scott	
DESIGNER(S)	
Steve Scott	
ART DIRECTOR	
Matthew Nadilo	
CLIENT	
NOTES	
Illustrator CS3, InDesign CS3; 300 gsm silk, matte laminated	

Ours Creative	003
DESIGN FIRM	SPECIMEN
David F. Moussallem	
DESIGNER(S)	
David F. Moussallem	
ART DIRECTOR	
Ours Creative	
CLIENT	
NOTES	
Illustrator CS3; Cougar 130 lb. Cover	

Louviere + Vanessa	004
DESIGN FIRM	SPECIMEN
Jeff Louviere	
DESIGNER(S)	
Jeff Louviere	
ART DIRECTOR	
Chris Rudge	
CLIENT	
NOTES	
Illustrator CS3; Chipboard; Letterpress	

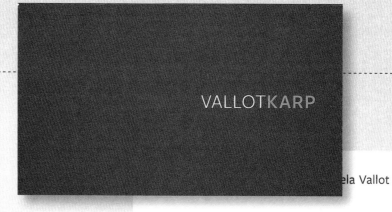

VALLOTKARP

...ela Vallot

VallotKarp
370 Riverside Drive #15E
New York, NY 10025

T (212) 222-0339
F (212) 222-0940
E avallot@vallotkarp.com

001

matthewnadilo
BDes, AdvDipIntDes
Interior Designer

61 (0)413 114 487
matt@matthewnadilo.com
matthewnadilo.com

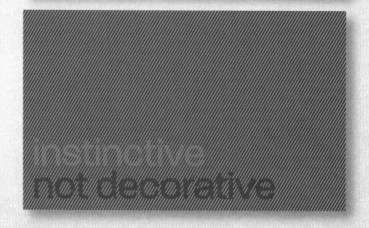

not decorative

002

003

OURS CREATIVE
DAVID MOUSSALLEM 214 ST. GEORGE STREET– 505 M5R 2N8
EMAIL OURSCREATIVE@GMAIL.COM TELEPHONE 1 905 616 2444

004

Loose Collective

Graham Jones
+44 (0)773 275 2698
gman@loosecollective.net

www.loosecollective.net

001

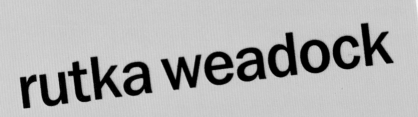

002

shoot pictures,
not people.

rainwaters

matt rainwaters | photographer
818 642 2056
matt@mattrainwaters.com
mattrainwaters.com

003

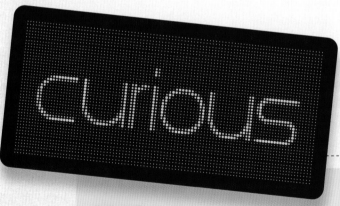

**Modern
Relaxed
Delicious**

Curious
35 Fitzroy Street, St Kilda
Reservations (03) 8530 8888
www.curiousatstkilda.com.au

004

G-Man	001
DESIGN FIRM	SPECIMEN
Graham Jones	
DESIGNER(S)	
Graham Jones	
ART DIRECTOR	
Graham Jones, Lee Garland, Chris Savage, Gary Peplof, Peggy Manning	
CLIENT	
NOTES	
Illustrator CS3; Letterpress in black on Luxury Matboard and Beer Matboard	

Rutka Weadock Design	002
DESIGN FIRM	SPECIMEN
Bora Shin	
DESIGNER(S)	
Anthony Rutka	
ART DIRECTOR	
Rutka Weadock Design	
CLIENT	
NOTES	
InDesign CS3; Strathmore Writing 130 lb.	

Cody Haltom	003
DESIGN FIRM	SPECIMEN
Cody Haltom	
DESIGNER(S)	
Cody Haltom	
ART DIRECTOR	
Matt Rainwaters	
CLIENT	
NOTES	
Illustrator CS3; Neenah Classic Crest Solar White 110 lb; C 2/2, embossed	

Steve Scott Graphic Design	004
DESIGN FIRM	SPECIMEN
Steve Scott	
DESIGNER(S)	
Steve Scott	
ART DIRECTOR	
ERDI Group	
CLIENT	
NOTES	
Illustrator CS3, InDesign CS3; 300 gsm silk, matte laminated	

Belinda Williams	*001*
DESIGN FIRM	SPECIMEN
Belinda Williams	
DESIGNER(S)	
Belinda Williams	
ART DIRECTOR	
Belinda Williams	
CLIENT	
NOTES	
Illustrator CS3; 310 gsm artboard, matte celloglaze	

G-Man	*002*
DESIGN FIRM	SPECIMEN
Graham Jones	
DESIGNER(S)	
Graham Jones	
ART DIRECTOR	
Peter Parry (Steranko)	
CLIENT	
NOTES	
Illustrator CS3; Letterpress in gold on heavy duty Box board	

*D*MNGOOD*	*003*
DESIGN FIRM	SPECIMEN
Dan Adler	
DESIGNER(S)	
Dan Adler	
ART DIRECTOR	
Stephanie Lemer	
CLIENT	
NOTES	
InDesign CS3; Strathmore Writing, White Wove	

Reactor	*004*
DESIGN FIRM	SPECIMEN
Chase Wilson	
DESIGNER(S)	
Clifton Alexander	
ART DIRECTOR	
A. L. Huber General Contractor	
CLIENT	
NOTES	
Classic Crest Recycleds	

BELINDA WILLIAMS
GRAPHIC DESIGNER
CELL**604.836.3243**
HELLO@BELINDAWILLIAMS.NET
FAX1.866.884.0477
WWW.BELINDAWILLIAMS.NET

⟵ THUMB GRIP REGION

Hello, I used to belong to a designer named Belinda Williams who has a slightly unusual Australian accent. She has given me to you so you can call her on 604.836.3243. Otherwise you can write to her at hello@belindawilliams.net.

☐ DESIGNER
☐ ARTIST
☐ FRIEND
☐ SNOWBOARDER

001

ster anko
Clothing For Men And Women

172 Burton Road
West Didsbury
Manchester
M20 1LH

T: 0161 448 0108
E: info@steranko.co.uk

www.steranko.co.uk

002

STEPHANIE LEMER **H** 301.941.1335 **M** 301.806.5052 STEPHANIELEMER@STARPOWER.NET

STEPHANIE

003

DEAN HUGGINS
project manager

913-341-4880 (xt 103)
816-506-9727 (cell)
dhuggins@alhuber.com

A.L. HUBER
GENERAL CONTRACTOR

ALHuber.com

10770 El Monte
Overland Park KS 66211

p **913-341-4880**   f **913-341-1940**

004

Penrith Conservatorium of Music
PO Box 2, Penrith NSW 2751
T 61 2 4723 7603 F 61 2 4731 3701
www.jspac.com.au

PCoM
Penrith Conservatorium of Music

Q

PP&VA
Penrith Performing Arts & Visual Arts Ltd

the Joan

001

MARK MINICUCCI
EXECUTIVE PRODUCER
1301 M STREET NW SUITE 1010
WASHINGTON DC USA 20005
T 202 683 8975 M 703 395 4386
MARK.MINICUCCI@DMNGOOD.COM

* A CREATIVE AGENCY

D*MNGOOD

002

003

004

Boccalatte | 001
DESIGN FIRM | SPECIMEN
Suzanne Boccalatte
DESIGNER(S)
Suzanne Boccalatte
ART DIRECTOR
Joan Sutherland Performing Arts Centre
CLIENT
NOTES
InDesign CS3, Illustrator CS3; Flouro Inks,
Sovereign Offset 300 gsm

D*MNGOOD | 002
DESIGN FIRM | SPECIMEN
Dan Adler
DESIGNER(S)
Dan Adler
ART DIRECTOR
D*MNGOOD
CLIENT
NOTES
InDesign CS3; Finch Fine Opaque Smooth

Dreambox Creative | 003
DESIGN FIRM | SPECIMEN
Matt Stuart
DESIGNER(S)
Doru Ghedeon Bere
ART DIRECTOR
Brand the Speaker
CLIENT
NOTES
Strathmore Writing Cover 110 lb.

Marc O'Brien | 004
DESIGN FIRM | SPECIMEN
Marc O'Brien
DESIGNER(S)
Marc O'Brien
ART DIRECTOR
Marc O'Brien
CLIENT
NOTES
Cougar Bright White 130 lb. Cover

Imagine
DESIGN FIRM
001
SPECIMEN

David Caunce
DESIGNER(S)

David Caunce
ART DIRECTOR

Barry White
CLIENT

NOTES
Quark, Illustrator CS3, Photoshop CS3; 300 gsm board, matte lamination

Iceberg
DESIGN FIRM
002
SPECIMEN

David Sampedro
DESIGNER(S)

David Sampedro, Ximena Riveros
ART DIRECTOR

CH Invest
CLIENT

NOTES
Illustrator CS3; curious skin paper black, 55 mm x 90mm – 380 gsm, Selective Glam

Mine
DESIGN FIRM
003
SPECIMEN

Christopher Simmons, Tim Belonax
DESIGNER(S)

Christopher Simmons
ART DIRECTOR

NRG
CLIENT

NOTES
Illustrator CS3; Mohawk Options 130 lb.

Iceberg
DESIGN FIRM
004
SPECIMEN

Ximena Riveros
DESIGNER(S)

David Sampedro, Ximena Riveros
ART DIRECTOR

Iceberg
CLIENT

NOTES
Illustrator CS3; curious skin paper black, 55 mm x 90 mm; Selective Glam 380 gsm, 5 fluo Pantone front/back

001

002

NICK @ EXPERIENCE**NRG**.COM

Nick James

Director of Business Development **NRG Marketing, LLC**

11912 W. WASHINGTON BLVD. LOS ANGELES, CA 90066

OFFICE LINE. 310 255 7995   FACSIMILE. 310 255 7996

Direct Line. 310 997 0778   *Cellular Line.* 310 403 8738

GREAT IDEAS
exceptional
experiences

NRG

CREATING MEANING
through
EXPERIENCE

NRG

003

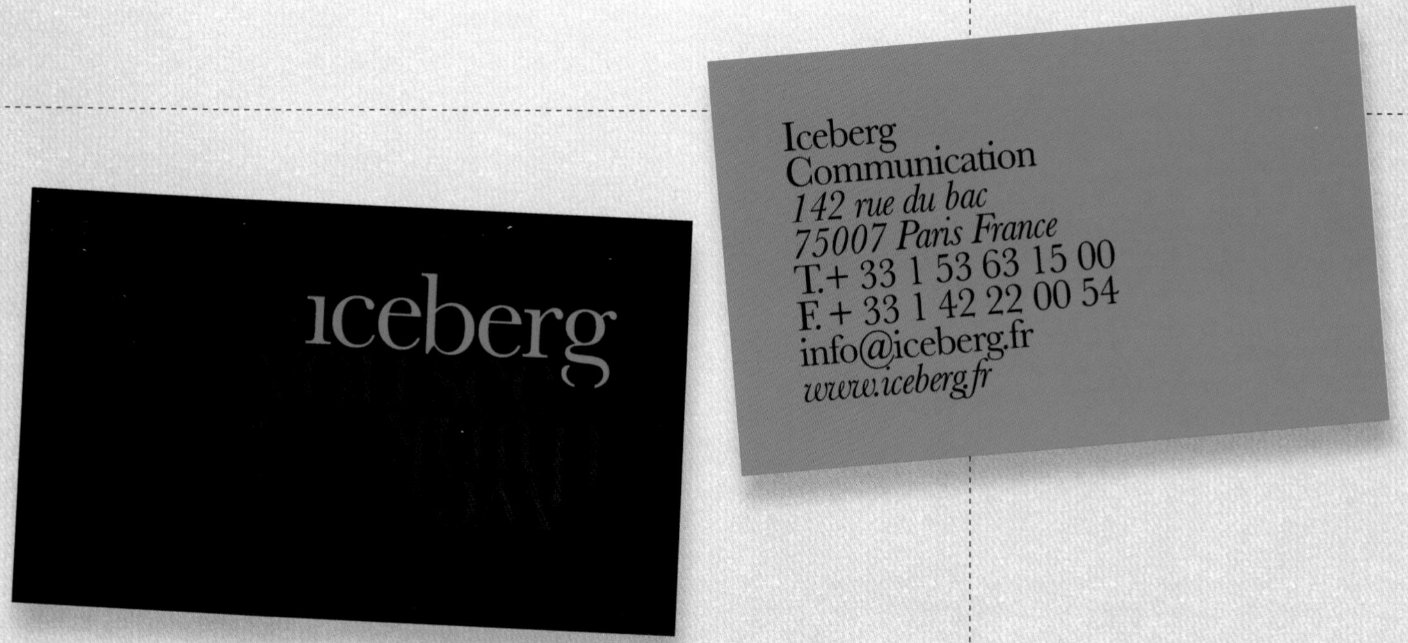

iceberg

Iceberg
Communication
142 rue du bac
75007 Paris France
T.+ 33 1 53 63 15 00
F. + 33 1 42 22 00 54
info@iceberg.fr
www.iceberg.fr

004

»West-MEC

Chris Cook Director of Marketing & PR
chris.cook@west-mec.org

Western Maricopa Education Center
4949 West Indian School Road
Phoenix, AZ 85031

p 623.435.4938
f 623.873.4188
www.west-mec.org

Welcome
to
West-MEC

001

ADMIT ONE

B2B/DFW
NETWORKING
LUNCHEON

Every 2nd and 4th Tuesday
11:30 am to 1:00 pm
Spaghetti Warehouse
at 15th and Central in Plano
RSVPs required

www.b2bdfw.com

Design: Bronson Ma Creative
www.bronsonma.com

002

003

004

Tomko Design	001
DESIGN FIRM	SPECIMEN
Mike Tomko	
DESIGNER(S)	
Mike Tomko	
ART DIRECTOR	
Tomko Design	
CLIENT	
NOTES	
Illustrator CS3; Classic Crest Smooth	

traciedesigns	002
DESIGN FIRM	SPECIMEN
Tracie Valentino	
DESIGNER(S)	
Mari the Studio	
CLIENT	
NOTES	
Quark; Strathmore Natural White Smooth 100 lb. coated 2 sides	

Biz-R	003
DESIGN FIRM	SPECIMEN
Paul Warren	
DESIGNER(S)	
Blair Thomson	
ART DIRECTOR	
Amanda Marsden	
CLIENT	

tomko
TD

— CREATIVE DIRECTOR —
MIKE TOMKO
MIKE@TOMKODESIGN.COM
— E.MAIL — ———— WEBSITE —

602 412 4002
6868 N 7TH AVENUE SUITE 210 PHOENIX AZ 85013

Identifying with you.

TD

001

mari
THE STUDIO

MARI SHERMAN

1997 POST ROAD, FAIRFIELD, CT 06824
p 203 255 2999 f 203 255 2996
e INFO@MARITHESTUDIO.COM

A MINOR CHANGE FOR A MAJOR DIFFERENCE.

MARITHESTUDIO.COM

002

I.D /

BT

Personal Data /
BLAIR THOMSON
CREATIVE DIRECTOR
BLAIR@BIZ-R.CO.UK
01803 868989

Logo /

bIZ-R

001

A

ADAM
FARRINGTON

504
914-6972

2514
SAINT CLAUDE AVE
NEW ORLEANS
LOUISIANA
70117

METAL
SCULPTURE

adam@adamfarrington.com

NEW
ORLEANS
LOUISIANA

70117

002

Compelling Interactive Media

Bellyfeel.

Bellyfeel Limited
110 Timber Wharf, Castlefield
Manchester, M15 4LD

T: +44 (0)161 832 1472
E: info@bellyfeel.co.uk
W: www.bellyfeel.co.uk

003

THE DESIGN WORKS GROUP.COM

TORREY SHARP PRINCIPAL + BUSINESS DIRECTOR
torrey@thedesignworksgroup.com • ext.1

TELEPHONE 541 549 1096 • FAX 541 549 1097
257 SOUTH PINE ST. • P.O. BOX 1773 SISTERS, OR 97759

004

Biz-R	001
DESIGN FIRM	SPECIMEN
Blair Thomson	
DESIGNER(S)	
Blair Thomson	
ART DIRECTOR	
Biz-R (US)	
CLIENT	
NOTES	
Quark, Illustrator Cs3 & Photoshop CS3; 400 gsm matte art stock	

Louviere + Vanessa	002
DESIGN FIRM	SPECIMEN
Jeff Louviere	
DESIGNER(S)	
Jeff Louviere	
ART DIRECTOR	
Adam Farrington	
CLIENT	
NOTES	
Illustrator CS3; Lettra, Letterpress	

G-Man	003
DESIGN FIRM	SPECIMEN
Graham Jones	
DESIGNER(S)	
Graham Jones	
ART DIRECTOR	
Krishna Stott, Andrew Lim (Bellyfeel)	
CLIENT	
NOTES	
Illustrator CS3; Letterpress in Pantone Process Blue and Silver mix on box board and Beer Matboard	

The Designworks Group	004
DESIGN FIRM	SPECIMEN
Jeff Miller	
DESIGNER(S)	
The Designworks Group	
CLIENT	

Clear Space	*001*
DESIGN FIRM	SPECIMEN
Will Hum	
DESIGNER(S)	
Will Hum	
ART DIRECTOR	
Main St. Psychological Centre	
CLIENT	
NOTES	
Illustrator CS3; Crane's	

TOKY Branding + Design	*002*
DESIGN FIRM	SPECIMEN
Eric Thoelke	
DESIGNER(S)	
Eric Thoelke	
ART DIRECTOR	
Grand Center, Inc.	
CLIENT	
NOTES	
CS3, Quark; Mohawk Superfine Ultrawhite	

Unfold Studio	*003*
DESIGN FIRM	SPECIMEN
Huw Briscoe	
DESIGNER(S)	
Huw Briscoe	
ART DIRECTOR	
Unfold Studio	
CLIENT	
NOTES	
InDesign CS3, Illustrator CS3; Various stocks duplexed	

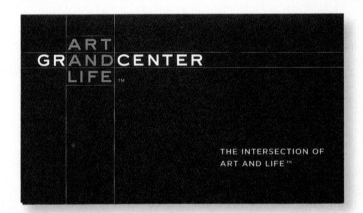

001

002

HUW BRISCOE
MISTD BA (HONS)

07929 802 892
HUW@UNFOLDSTUDIO.COM
WWW.UNFOLDSTUDIO.COM

UNIQUOUS SHAPIUM

- DON'T FIT INTO ROLODEXES
- DIE CUT
- SOMETIMES BENDY
- PROUD OF THEIR UNIQUENESS
- HARD TO FORGET

KEY CHARACTERISTICS

In an ecosystem where many examples of *Cardious de Business* are anatomically similar, one genus stands out from the others. *Uniquous Shapium* calls attention to itself by evolving away from the traditional form to differentiate them from their competition. These evolved forms vary in size and shape and are believed to have stemmed from the ever-increasing need to stand out in order to attract a business mate. We have gathered some of the finest specimens to exhibit in this space.

NOTES

THE
NEW ZEALAND
CHEESE SCHOOL
LIMITED.

SEVEN GREEN

Christopher Bing
Dental Surgeon BDS (Otago)

cp bing dental surgery ltd

223 Main Road
Tawa
Wellington 5028
New Zealand
Tel: +64 4 232 7146
Fax: +64 4 232 6611
bingdental@paradise.net.nz

bingdental

GRETCHEN WESTBROCK

DESIGNER / ART DIRECTOR
(612) 279.2390 gretchen@adsoka.com

DAVIDSON
D E S I G N S

SUZY DAVIDSON
INTERIOR | COLOR | FLORAL

suzy@davidson-designs.com

2737 ANDREWS AVE | BATAVIA, IL 60510
630 849 8245

davidson-designs.com

teton
marketing partners

Dynamic Ideas. Peak Results.

Denise Horton | Principal

3753 South Summit Lane
Evergreen, Colorado 80439
720.937.8978
denise@tetonmarketingpartners.com

TEN26DESIGN.COM

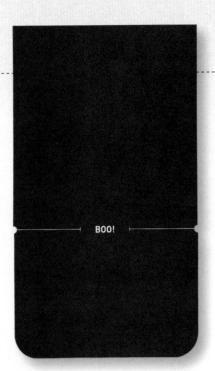

apparition STUDIO

Erica Feriozzi | Studio Manager

E erica@apparitionstudio.com

T/F **410**.853.7389   **410**.323.4113

W apparitionstudio.com

1425 Clarkview Road, Suite 600
Baltimore, MD 21209

BOO!

001

002

003

EUROPEAN ANTIQUE FINDS
www.forethome.com

AMY MARVER

tel 612 920 0221
amy@forethome.com
5816 dupont avenue south
minneapolis mn 55419 USA

004

Siquis	001
DESIGN FIRM	SPECIMEN
Greg Bennett	
DESIGNER(S)	
Greg Bennett	
ART DIRECTOR	
Apparition Studio	
CLIENT	
NOTES	
Illustrator CS3, InDesign CS3; Printed front and back with die cuts on Mohawk Superfine paper	

Archrival	002
DESIGN FIRM	SPECIMEN
Joel Kreutzer	
DESIGNER(S)	
Clint! Runge	
ART DIRECTOR	
Solas Distillery	
CLIENT	
NOTES	
Metal	

tmarks design	003
DESIGN FIRM	SPECIMEN
Terry Marks	
DESIGNER(S)	
Terry Marks	
ART DIRECTOR	
The Showbox	
CLIENT	
NOTES	
Freehand	

AFFINA	004
DESIGN FIRM	SPECIMEN
Jessica Zubrzycki	
DESIGNER(S)	
Renita Van Dusen	
ART DIRECTOR	
Forét	
CLIENT	
NOTES	
Illustrator CS3; Letterpress on watercolor paper	

Glitschka Studios	001
DESIGN FIRM	SPECIMEN
Von Glitschka	
DESIGNER(S)	
Von Glitschka	
ART DIRECTOR	
Mardi Gras World	
CLIENT	
NOTES	
Illustrator CS3; Classic Crest	

Glitschka Studios	002
DESIGN FIRM	SPECIMEN
Von Glitschka	
DESIGNER(S)	
Von Glitschka	
ART DIRECTOR	
Blaine Kern Studios	
CLIENT	
NOTES	
Illustrator CS3; Classic Crest	

P22 Type Foundry	003
DESIGN FIRM	SPECIMEN
Richard Kegler	
DESIGNER(S)	
Richard Kegler	
ART DIRECTOR	
Monika Paulikova	
CLIENT	
NOTES	
Letterpress, Hand set with vintage block on reclaimed smooth stock	

Di Depux	004
DESIGN FIRM	SPECIMEN
Despina Bournele	
DESIGNER(S)	
Despina Bournele	
ART DIRECTOR	
Paul Bourneles-Christina Samara	
CLIENT	
NOTES	
Illustrator CS3; 1 Pantone 300 gsm. Curious Metallics, Die Cut	

001

002

003

004

001

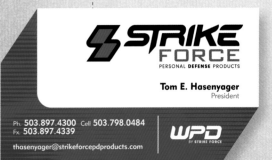

002

003

004

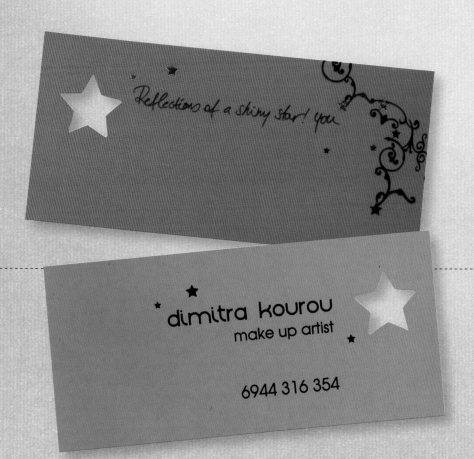

005

BBM&D Strategic Branding | 001
DESIGN FIRM | SPECIMEN

Barbara Brown
DESIGNER(S)

Barbara Brown
ART DIRECTOR

The Genius Organization
CLIENT

NOTES
Illustrator CS3; Stainless steel

Glitschka Studios | 002
DESIGN FIRM | SPECIMEN

Von Glitschka
DESIGNER(S)

Von Glitschka
ART DIRECTOR

Strike Force
CLIENT

NOTES
Illustrator CS3, Photoshop CS3; Classic Crest

Glitschka Studios | 003
DESIGN FIRM | SPECIMEN

Von Glitschka
DESIGNER(S)

Von Glitschka
ART DIRECTOR

Myows
CLIENT

NOTES
Illustrator CS3; Classic Crest

Bronson Ma Creative | 004
DESIGN FIRM | SPECIMEN

Bronson Ma
DESIGNER(S)

Bronson Ma
ART DIRECTOR

Fain Models
CLIENT

NOTES
Illustrator CS3

Di Depux | 005
DESIGN FIRM | SPECIMEN

Despina Bournele
DESIGNER(S)

Despina Bournele
ART DIRECTOR

Dimitra Kourou
CLIENT

NOTES
Illustrator CS3; 2 Pantones, Die Cut, Zanders Chromolux
250 gsm

Glitschka Studios	001
DESIGN FIRM	SPECIMEN
Von Glitschka	
DESIGNER(S)	
Von Glitschka	
ART DIRECTOR	
Fitness Experience	
CLIENT	
NOTES	
Illustrator CS3, Photoshop CS3; Classic Crest	

Lloyds Graphic Design Ltd.	002
DESIGN FIRM	SPECIMEN
Alexander Lloyd	
DESIGNER(S)	
Alexander Lloyd	
ART DIRECTOR	
New Zealand Extracts Ltd.	
CLIENT	
NOTES	
Freehand MX; Matte board 220 gsm	

FUNNEL: Eric Kass : Utilitarian + Commercial + Fine : Art	003
DESIGN FIRM	SPECIMEN
Eric Kass	
DESIGNER(S)	
Stillmotion Photo + Cinema	
CLIENT	
NOTES	
Illustrator; Silver letterpress, die-cut label	

Wicked Creative	004
DESIGN FIRM	SPECIMEN
Gabriel Garcia	
DESIGNER(S)	
Gabriel Garcia	
ART DIRECTOR	
Cathouse	
CLIENT	
NOTES	
Illustrator CS3; Classic Crest, duplex	

FITNESS
EXPERIENCE

www.RebuildReviveRenew.com

001

FITNESS
EXPERIENCE

Sherry Blackman
Owner

Fitness Experience
1715 Hill St SE
Albany, OR 97322
PO Box 1086 • Albany, OR 97321

info@rebuildreviverenew.com
PH. **541.917.3488**
FX. **541.917.3888**

**new zealand
extracts limited**

STEVE ANDERSON | ENGINEERING MANAGER

PO BOX 549 / BLENHEIM / NEW ZEALAND

T: +64 3 579 3399 / **F**: +64 3 579 3398

M: 021 734 709 / **E**: steve@nzextracts.co.nz

www.**nzextracts**.co.nz

002

647 477 5308 TORONTO ONTARIO CANADA
STILLMOTION.CA

patrick moreau
CINEMATOGRAPHER
PATRICK@STILLMOTION.CA

STILLMOTION
photo + cinema

003

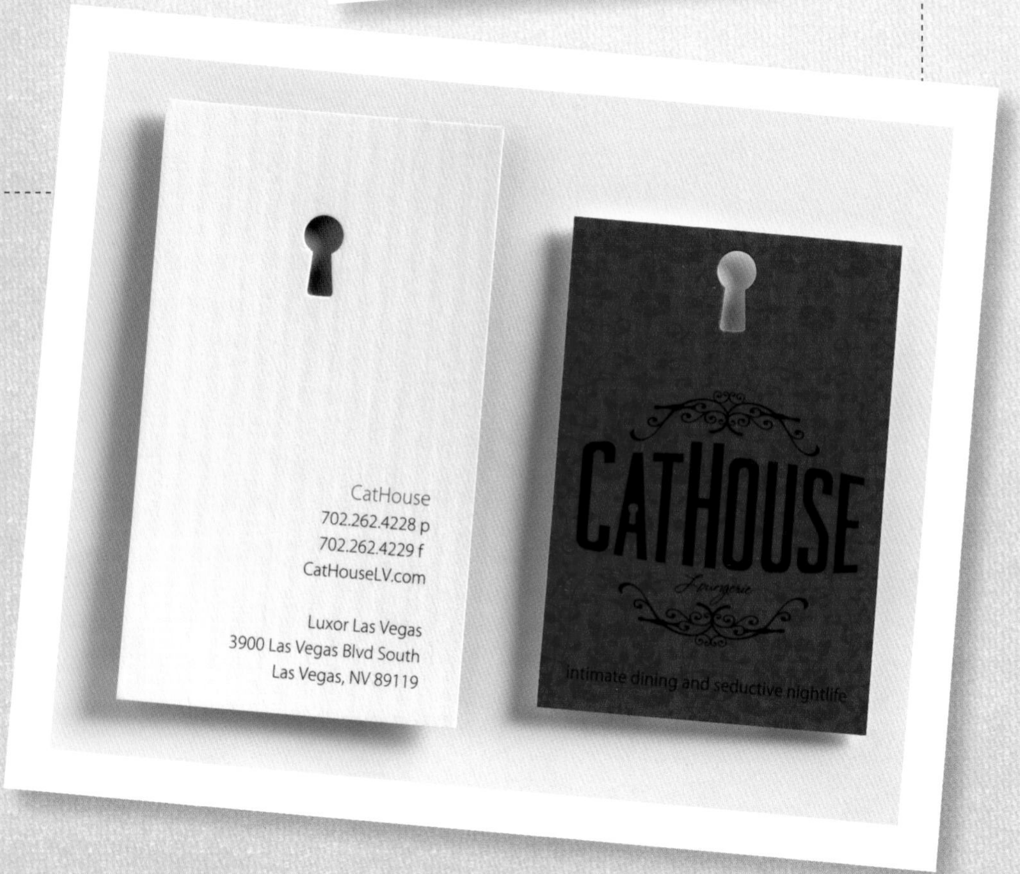

CatHouse
702.262.4228 p
702.262.4229 f
CatHouseLV.com

Luxor Las Vegas
3900 Las Vegas Blvd South
Las Vegas, NV 89119

CatHouse
Lingerie

intimate dining and seductive nightlife

004

terry**MARKS**design

aj parga-andrade   aj@tmarksdesign.com

94 pike street suite 36
seattle, washington 98101
VOICE 206 628.6427
FAX 206 628.6428

001

Jessica ZUBRZYCKI
DESIGNER

JESSICA@AFFINADESIGN.COM

AFFINADESIGN.COM   651 644 2889 W
763 412 8856 C

991 SELBY AVENUE
SAINT PAUL, MN 55104

affina
DESIGN IN THE LANGUAGE OF THE MARKETPLACE

002

Christopher Bing

Dental Surgeon BDS (Otago)

cp bing dental surgery ltd

223 Main Road
Tawa
Wellington 5028
New Zealand
Tel: +64 4 232 7146
Fax: +64 4 232 6611
bingdental@paradise.net.nz

bingdental

003

DARKEN

MICHAEL VICTOR
Darken Studios Recording & Design

390 Queens Quay W. Suite 614 Toronto, ON M5V 3A6
647.202.2424 | michael@darken.ca | www.darkenstudios.ca

004

tmarks design		001
DESIGN FIRM		SPECIMEN
Terry Marks		
DESIGNER(S)		
Terry Marks		
ART DIRECTOR		
tmarks design		
CLIENT		
NOTES		
InDesign CS3; Durotone, Butcher White 80 lb., engraved		

AFFINA		002
DESIGN FIRM		SPECIMEN
Jessica Zubrzycki		
DESIGNER(S)		
Renita Van Dusen		
ART DIRECTOR		
AFFINA		
CLIENT		
NOTES		
Illustrator CS3		

Lloyds Graphic Design Ltd.		003
DESIGN FIRM		SPECIMEN
Alexander Lloyd		
DESIGNER(S)		
Alexander Lloyd		
ART DIRECTOR		
Bing Dental		
CLIENT		
NOTES		
Freehand MX; Matte art board 220 gsm		

Darken Studios		004
DESIGN FIRM		SPECIMEN
David F. Moussallem		
DESIGNER(S)		
David F. Moussallem		
ART DIRECTOR		
Darken Studios		
CLIENT		
NOTES		
Illustrator CS3; Cougar Cover 130 lb.		

Timber Design Company Inc.
DESIGN FIRM

001
SPECIMEN

Lars Lawson
ART DIRECTOR

3rd Eye Records & Management
CLIENT

NOTES

Freehand, QuarkXPress; Starwhite Smooth 110 lb.

Afterhours Group
DESIGN FIRM

002
SPECIMEN

Fedra Carina Meredith
DESIGNER(S)

Fedra Carina Meredith
ART DIRECTOR

Teton Marketing Partners
CLIENT

NOTES

Illustrator CS3, InDesign CS3; 3/2, custom die cut;
Neenah Classic Crest

HI(NY), LLC
DESIGN FIRM

003
SPECIMEN

Hitomi Watanabe, Iku Oyamada
DESIGNER(S)

Hitomi Watanabe, Iku Oyamada
ART DIRECTOR

fLorEsta
CLIENT

NOTES

Illustrator CS3; Double-mounted matte paper

001

002

[juan carlo bermudez]

floral designer

917 612 4446

carlo@florestanyc.com

www.florestanyc.com

[fLo rE sta]

[fLo rE sta]

[COUNTER

[COUNTER]FORM

WE
THINK
INSIDE
OUT.

KURT
SABERI

10934
SW
CELESTE
LANE
UNIT 403

PORTLAND
OREGON
97225
USA

T 503
747
8765

KURT@
COUNTERFORM.
US

001

Charlie Palmer
1530 Main Street, Dallas, TX 75201
t 214.261.4600 f 214.261.4605
www.charliepalmer.com

CHARLIE
PALMER

002

Sherrie Mitchell
Sales Director

sherrie@reelcentric.com

m | + 850 554_0879

reelcentric.com
Office: + 850 434 1244
Facsimile: + 850 434 2270

3 W. Garden St., Suite 370
Pensacola, FL 32502

003

303 N. Sweetzer Ave.

Los Angeles, CA | 90048

T:323.852.8979 | F:323.852.1727

www.matchcreative.com

Jennifer Morrison MATCH CREATIVE TALENT

Jmorrison@matchcreative.com

MATCH
CREATIVE TALENT

004

Counterform	001
DESIGN FIRM	SPECIMEN
Kurt Saberi	
DESIGNER(S)	
Kurt Saberi	
ART DIRECTOR	
Counterform	
CLIENT	
NOTES	

InDesign CS3; Pegasus Midnight Black,
Crane's Palette, red

Mirko Ilic Corp.	002
DESIGN FIRM	SPECIMEN
Mirko Ilic	
DESIGNER(S)	
Mirko Ilic	
ART DIRECTOR	
Charlie Palmer Group	
CLIENT	
NOTES	

Illustrator CS3

Chen Design Associates	003
DESIGN FIRM	SPECIMEN
Jure Gavran	
DESIGNER(S)	
Joshua Chen / Laurie Carrigan	
ART DIRECTOR	
Reel Centric	
CLIENT	
NOTES	

Illustrator CS3; Strathmore Soft White Wove 110 lb. Cover

Geyrhalter Design	004
DESIGN FIRM	SPECIMEN
Boby Dragulescu	
DESIGNER(S)	
Fabian Geyrhalter	
ART DIRECTOR	
Match Creative Talent	
CLIENT	
NOTES	

InDesign CS3; Neenah Classic Crest, 110 lb.
Smooth Solar White

The Creative Method
DESIGN FIRM
001
SPECIMEN

Tony Ibbotson
DESIGNER(S)

Tony Ibbotson
ART DIRECTOR

The New Zealand Cheese School Limited
CLIENT

NOTES

Illustrator CS3; Sovereign Offset 300 gsm
from K.W. Doggett

Flávio Carvalho
DESIGN FIRM
002
SPECIMEN

Flávio Carvalho
DESIGNER(S)

Flávio Carvalho
ART DIRECTOR

Cacá Fotografia Infantil
CLIENT

NOTES

Matte 240 gsm, matte lamination, Reserved
lamination film

Louviere + Vanessa
DESIGN FIRM
003
SPECIMEN

Jeff Louviere
DESIGNER(S)

Jeff Louviere
ART DIRECTOR

Cindy Keuffer
CLIENT

NOTES

Illustrator CS3; Speckletone, Letterpress

Honest Bros.
DESIGN FIRM
004
SPECIMEN

Eric Hines, Ryan Lee
DESIGNER(S)

Honest Bros.
CLIENT

NOTES

CS3; Neenah Classic Columns Duplex, Avery Peel & Stick

**THE
NEW ZEALAND
CHEESE SCHOOL
LIMITED.**

33 Tirau Street   **P +64 7 8838 238**
Putaruru 3411   **F +64 7 8838 235**

E office@newzealandcheeseschool.co.nz
www.newzealandcheeseschool.co.nz

001

002

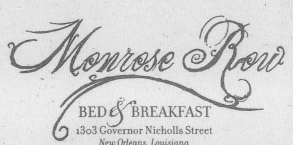

003

004

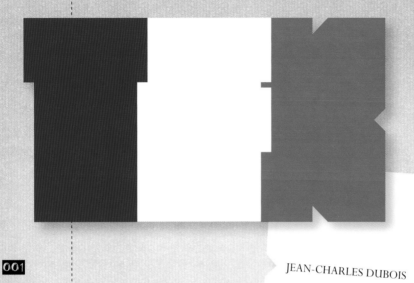

001

JEAN-CHARLES DUBOIS

THE FRENCH KITCHEN

7 Magazine Road,
#01-03 Central Mall,
Singapore 059572

T. 65-6438 1823
F. 65-6438 3043
M.65-9768 1070
E. jean-charles@thefrenchkitchen.com.sg
W. www.thefrenchkitchen.com.sg

ready_aim_launch

LAUNCAGENTS

STEVEN R JAMBOR_CEO
370 POPLAR WINNETKA IL 60093
773.263.9962
STEVE@LAUNCAGENTS.COM

002

*ready_* a robust discovery process to identify strategic
market opportunities. *aim_* leadership to pull mission critical
products through the development funnel in the shortest
amount of time. *launch_* vision to propel products into the
market with a trajectory to exceed expectations.

FORM.
FUNCTION.
FINISH

MARK WILSON

248.981.9094
mark@markjwilson.com

markjwilson.com

003

Rehybrid	001
DESIGN FIRM	SPECIMEN
Tomaz Goh	
DESIGNER(S)	
Tomaz Goh	
ART DIRECTOR	
The French Kitchen by Jean-Charles Dubois	
CLIENT	
NOTES	
Illustrator CS3; Conqueror Wove Brilliant White	

sparc, inc.	002
DESIGN FIRM	SPECIMEN
Richard Cassis	
DESIGNER(S)	
Richard Cassis	
ART DIRECTOR	
Launch Agents	
CLIENT	
NOTES	
Illustrator CS3, InDesign; Fibermark Touché, Black/White Duplex Cover	

Spark! Communications	003
DESIGN FIRM	SPECIMEN
Sherri Lawton	
DESIGNER(S)	
Sherri Lawton	
ART DIRECTOR	
Mark Wilson	
CLIENT	
NOTES	
Illustrator CS3; Cougar paper, laser die cut	

3rd Edge Communications	001
DESIGN FIRM	SPECIMEN
Nick Schmitz	
DESIGNER(S)	
Frankie Gonzalez	
ART DIRECTOR	
George Fontenette	
CLIENT	
NOTES	
InDesign CS3	

InsaneFacilities	002
DESIGN FIRM	SPECIMEN
Jarek Berecki	
DESIGNER(S)	
Jarek Berecki	
ART DIRECTOR	
Seven Green Promotion	
CLIENT	
NOTES	
Illustrator CS3; 230 gsm paper, double-sided matte lamination	

Timber Design Company Inc.	003
DESIGN FIRM	SPECIMEN
Lars Lawson	
ART DIRECTOR	
Mirror Mirror Hair Design	
CLIENT	
NOTES	
Freehand; 110 lb. Starwhite Vellum	

squarehand.com	004
DESIGN FIRM	SPECIMEN
Monica Torrejón Kelly	
DESIGNER(S)	
Monica Torrejón Kelly	
ART DIRECTOR	
Shout Out! Clothing	
CLIENT	
NOTES	
Illustrator CS3; Couche Plastified Matte, spot varnish	

001

002

MICHAEL ALDRICH
STYLIST

YOUR APPOINTMENT WITH MICHAEL

MIRROR ЯOЯЯIM
MIRRORMIRRORHAIRDESIGN.COM
230 E NINTH ST . SUITE 101
INDIANAPOLIS . IN 46204

317.258.6453

003

Colin Egglesfield
shoutoutclothing.com
315 Bleecker st. suite 350
NY, NY 10014
colin@shoutoutclothing.com
t.212.620.7670 f.208.445.9469

Shout Out!

spell it out.

 004

FM

FM

Fusedmedia
9544 5114
0438 421 093
inbox@fusedmedia.com.au
www.fusedmedia.com.au

PO Box 2611
Taren Point
NSW 2229

001

2257 Vantage St.
Dallas, Texas 75207

214.744.0555 tel
214.744.0577 fax

866.624.2040
rangeUS.com

RANGE

John Swieter
founder / design director   john@rangeus.com

002

GINA GHURA / Innovation Consultant

464 Old South Head Road Rose Bay NSW 2029
M 0410 495 675   E gina@eightinnovation.com

GINA GHURA / eight innovation
creative thinking for commercial solutions
reach me on 0410 495 675
or write me an email
gina@eightinnovation.com

003

Fusedmedia		001
DESIGN FIRM		SPECIMEN
Jared Fusedale		
DESIGNER(S)		
Jared Fusedale		
ART DIRECTOR		
Fusedmedia		
CLIENT		
NOTES		
Illustrator CS3, InDesign CS3		

Range		002
DESIGN FIRM		SPECIMEN
John Swieter		
DESIGNER(S)		
John Swieter		
ART DIRECTOR		
Range		
CLIENT		
NOTES		
InDesign CS3; Starwhite Vicksburg		

The Creative Method		003
DESIGN FIRM		SPECIMEN
Andi Yanto		
DESIGNER(S)		
Tony Ibbotson		
ART DIRECTOR		
Eight Innovation		
CLIENT		
NOTES		
Illustrator CS3; Knight Vellum 280 gsm from K.W. Doggett		

wp2 design	001
DESIGN FIRM	SPECIMEN
Willis Porter	
DESIGNER(S)	
Willis Porter	
ART DIRECTOR	
wp2 design	
CLIENT	
NOTES	
InDesign CS3; 16-pt. Snow White	

Voicebox Creative	002
DESIGN FIRM	SPECIMEN
Dylan Schepers	
DESIGNER(S)	
Jacques Rossouw	
ART DIRECTOR	
Voicebox Creative	
CLIENT	
NOTES	
Illustrator CS3; Mohawk Superfine	

Andru Creative	003
DESIGN FIRM	SPECIMEN
Andrew Suggit	
ART DIRECTOR	
CRU/Digital	
CLIENT	
NOTES	
Illustrator CS3, InDesign CS3; Knight White	

2

Willis Porter
Graphic Designer

wp2 design
2225 Abergeldie Drive
Memphis, TN 38119

901.277.7911 | Phone
willis@wp2design.com

wp2design.com

001

w|p²

VOICEBOX
CREATIVE

BUILDING BRANDS
THAT SPEAK VOLUMES

Jacques Rossouw
Managing Partner
Creative Director

Voicebox Creative, Inc.
Three Meacham Place
San Francisco, CA 94109

t 415 674 3211
f 415 674 5616
jacques@voiceboxsf.com

www.voiceboxsf.com

002

NICOLE LEATHERBY/FINANCE MANAGER
nicole@crudigital.com.au

....

cru/digital.
level 1, 232 arthur st
newstead, q 4006

www.**crudigital**.com.au

T   + 61 7 3358 6845
F   + 61 7 3105 7311

cru/digital.

003

001

002

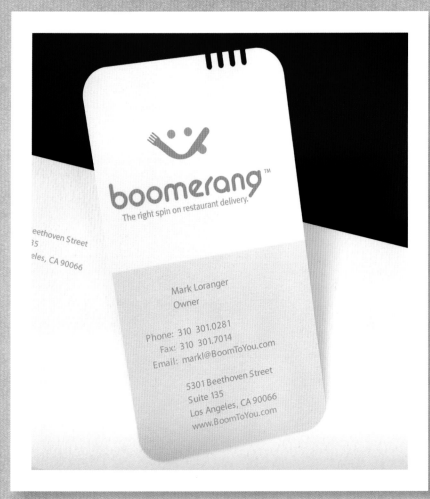

003

004

Cody Haltom	001
DESIGN FIRM	SPECIMEN
Cody Haltom	
DESIGNER(S)	
Cody Haltom	
ART DIRECTOR	
The TenCount Foundation	
CLIENT	
NOTES	
Illustrator CS3; French Construction Tile Green 100 lb. coated, 2/2, blind foil stamp, perforation	

Pink Blue Black & Orange Co., Ltd.	002
DESIGN FIRM	SPECIMEN
Nuttapol Nantasukasame	
DESIGNER(S)	
Punlarp Punnotok	
ART DIRECTOR	
Color Party Object Co., Ltd.	
CLIENT	
NOTES	
Illustrator 10	

Evenson Design Group	003
DESIGN FIRM	SPECIMEN
Mark Sojka	
DESIGNER(S)	
Stan Evenson	
ART DIRECTOR	
Boomerang	
CLIENT	
NOTES	
Illustrator CS3; Classic Crest Solar White	

christiansen : creative	004
DESIGN FIRM	SPECIMEN
Tricia Christiansen	
DESIGNER(S)	
Tricia Christiansen	
ART DIRECTOR	
St. Croix Souvenir Company	
CLIENT	
NOTES	
Letterpress	

| A3 Design | 001 |
| DESIGN FIRM | SPECIMEN |

Alan Altman
DESIGNER(S)

Amanda Altman
ART DIRECTOR

Armando Bellmas Photographer
CLIENT

NOTES

Illustrator CS3; 2x thick Classic Crest 130 lb.

| Ten26 Design Group | 002 |
| DESIGN FIRM | SPECIMEN |

Tony Demakis
DESIGNER(S)

Tony Demakis
ART DIRECTOR

Ten26 Design Group
CLIENT

NOTES

Illustrator CS3; 110 lb. Cover, Strathmore writing, wove finish, die cut

| AD Grafica & Comunicazione | 003 |
| DESIGN FIRM | SPECIMEN |

Giancarlo Salvador
DESIGNER(S)

Giancarlo Salvador
ART DIRECTOR

Brand SRL
CLIENT

NOTES

Illustrator CS3

| 3rd Edge Communications | 004 |
| DESIGN FIRM | SPECIMEN |

Nick Schmitz
DESIGNER(S)

Frankie Gonzalez
ART DIRECTOR

Eden Organix
CLIENT

001

002

BRAND SRL
36040 Torri di Quartesolo (VI) - Italy
Via Brescia 31
Tel. +39.0444.267014
Fax. +39.0444.267302

Paolo Ferrari - Mobile: +39.392.4700282 - ferrari@brandsrl.net

003

BRAND

REAL ESTATE

DONNA SPINELLI
spa director

store

spa

reach

EDEN ORGANIX.COM

215 RARITAN AVENUE, HIGHLAND PARK, NJ 08904

888 907 EDEN

SPA DIRECTOR @ EDEN ORGANIX.COM

eden
organix

ECO-CONSCIOUS BEAUTY
EDEN ORGANIX'S GUIDING MISSION IS TO ENRICH THE LIVES OF
OUR CLIENTS WITH ORGANIC, NATURAL, AND ECO-ESSENTIAL
BASED PRODUCTS AND SERVICES. *edenorganix.com*

004

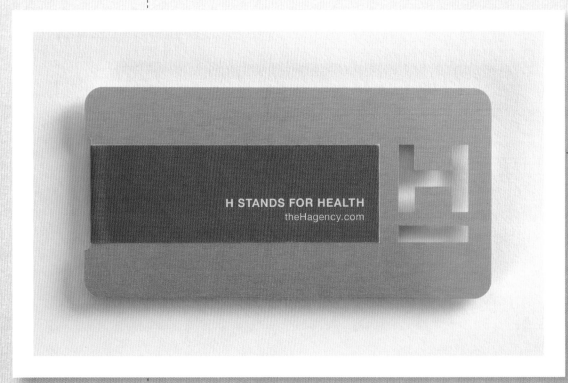

002

003

The H Agency	001
DESIGN FIRM	SPECIMEN
Jason Graham	
DESIGNER(S)	
Winnie Hart	
ART DIRECTOR	
The H Agency	
CLIENT	
NOTES	
Metal card, pressure-sensitive label	

Shelby Designs & Illustrates	002
DESIGN FIRM	SPECIMEN
Will Yang	
DESIGNER(S)	
Shelby Putnam Tupper	
ART DIRECTOR	
The Studios SF	
CLIENT	
NOTES	
InDesign CS3, Illustrator CS3; Neenah Environment	

Evenson Design Group	003
DESIGN FIRM	SPECIMEN
Angela Kim	
DESIGNER(S)	
Stan Evenson, Mark Sojka	
ART DIRECTOR	
Now Cafe	
CLIENT	
NOTES	
Illustrator CS3; Classic Crest	

Rule29 Creative DESIGN FIRM	001 SPECIMEN
Kara Ayaram DESIGNER(S)	
Justin Ahrens ART DIRECTOR	
Davidson Designs CLIENT	
NOTES	
InDesign CS3	

Miriello Grafico DESIGN FIRM	002 SPECIMEN
Dennis Garcia DESIGNER(S)	
Ron Miriello ART DIRECTOR	
Miriello Grafico CLIENT	
NOTES	
Illustrator CS3, InDesign CS3; Mohawk vellum, *French construction*	

Adsoka DESIGN FIRM	003 SPECIMEN
Gretchen Westbrock DESIGNER(S)	
Adsoka CLIENT	
NOTES	
Illustrator CS3; French paper	

DEI Creative DESIGN FIRM	004 SPECIMEN
Noah Bell DESIGNER(S)	
Sara Green ART DIRECTOR	
GTS Development CLIENT	
NOTES	
InDesign CS3; Mohawk Options, custom die cut	

DAVIDSON

D E S I G N S

SUZY DAVIDSON

INTERIOR | COLOR | FLORAL

suzy@davidson-designs.com

2737 ANDREWS AVE | BATAVIA, IL 60510

630 849 8245

davidson-designs.com

001

MIRIELLO GRAFICO

Tracy Meiners
tracym@miriellografico.com

1660 LOGAN AVENUE
SAN DIEGO · CALIFORNIA 92113
619.234.1124 / TEL 1960 / FAX

WWW.MIRIELLOGRAFICO.COM   / brand expression

002

003

004

GLENN GOBEL

CUSTOM FRAMES

562 Lighthouse Avenue
Pacific Grove, CA 93950
telephone 831 372 7766
facsimile 831 372 7787
glenn@ggcustomframes.com

ggcustomframes.com

001

RDQ LUS
CREATIVE

FUNCTIONAL ART WORKS.

002

STEVE GORDON JR
designer/consultant/get-away driver

402.2120108
steve.g@rdqlus.com
www.rdqlus.com

JeTalia
1155 Camino Del Mar #453
Del Mar, CA 92014

T 858 481 0292 / 877 JeTalia
F 858 509 0281
E info@jetalia.com
W jetalia.com

003

Studio Conover	001
DESIGN FIRM	SPECIMEN
Nate Yates	
DESIGNER(S)	
David Conover	
ART DIRECTOR	
Glen Gobel Custom Frames	
CLIENT	
NOTES	
Classic Crest ABW Dt Cover, die cut	

RDQLUS Creative	002
DESIGN FIRM	SPECIMEN
Steve Gordon Jr.	
DESIGNER(S)	
Steve Gordon Jr.	
ART DIRECTOR	
RDQLUS Creative	
CLIENT	
NOTES	
Illustrator CS3, InDesign CS3; Georgia-Pacific standard 110 lb. uncoated card stock, duplexed, hand assembled	

Type G	003
DESIGN FIRM	SPECIMEN
Mike Nelson	
DESIGNER(S)	
Mike Nelson	
ART DIRECTOR	
JeTalia	
CLIENT	
NOTES	
Illustrator CS3; Curious Gold Leaf, laser cutting	

Plazma Design	*001*
DESIGN FIRM	SPECIMEN
Todd Hansson	
DESIGNER(S)	
Todd Hansson	
ART DIRECTOR	
Anthony McNamara	
CLIENT	
NOTES	
Illustrator CS3; Impress Silk, 350 gsm	
CMYK, Celloglazed	

Extra Credit Projects	*002*
DESIGN FIRM	SPECIMEN
Nolan Abney	
DESIGNER(S)	
Rob Jackson	
ART DIRECTOR	
Downpour	
CLIENT	
NOTES	
Cougar 120 lb.	

Clif Bar & Company	*003*
DESIGN FIRM	SPECIMEN
Leif Arneson + Matthew Loyd	
DESIGNER(S)	
Matthew Loyd	
ART DIRECTOR	
Clif Bar & Company	
CLIENT	
NOTES	
Illustrator CS3; FSC Certified	
100% postconsumer fiber content	

Element	*004*
DESIGN FIRM	SPECIMEN
Jeremy Slagle, Meg Russell	
DESIGNER(S)	
John McCollum	
ART DIRECTOR	
Element	
CLIENT	
NOTES	
CS3; French Pop-tone	

001

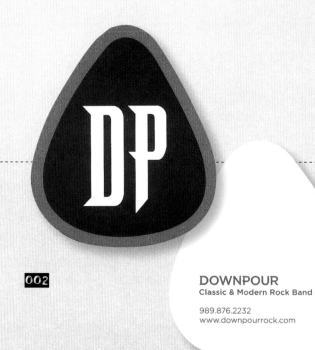

002

Leif Eric Arneson
SENIOR DESIGN LEAD

larneson@clifbar.com
T 510.558.7855 x611
C 415.286.6129
F 510.524.2293

1610 FIFTH STREET
BERKELEY, CA 94710
CLIFBAR.COM

003

004

Walter D. Man walter@hathead.com

HatHead.

Make your head happy™ hathead.com

001

PLAZMA

002

TODD HANSSON 0401134626 TH@PLAZMADESIGN.COM.AU

CAPTAIN MIKE JARVIS

0417 727 532

PTERODACTYL™

HELICOPTERS

003

CAPTAIN MIKE JARVIS
DIRECTOR + CHIEF PILOT
CPL(H) CERT MECH ENG(QIT)

PO Box 7012 Mt Crosby
Queensland 4306 Australia
TELEPHONE +617 3201 0005
FACSIMILE +617 3201 2888
EMAIL mike@pterodactylhelicopters.com.au
WEB www.pterodactylhelicopters.com.au

PTERODACTYL™
HELICOPTERS

004

Rule29 Creative	001
DESIGN FIRM	SPECIMEN
Josh Jensen	
DESIGNER(S)	
Justin Ahrens	
ART DIRECTOR	
Hathead	
CLIENT	
NOTES	
InDesign CS3	

Plazma Design	002
DESIGN FIRM	SPECIMEN
Todd Hansson	
DESIGNER(S)	
Todd Hansson	
ART DIRECTOR	
Plazma Design	
CLIENT	
NOTES	
Illustrator CS3; Expression Super Smooth 350 gsm, 2 PMS	

Plazma Design	003
DESIGN FIRM	SPECIMEN
Todd Hansson	
DESIGNER(S)	
Todd Hansson	
ART DIRECTOR	
Pterodactyl Helicopter	
CLIENT	
NOTES	
Illustrator CS3; Expression Super Smooth 350 gsm, 2 PMS	

Spring	004
DESIGN FIRM	SPECIMEN
Perry Chua	
DESIGNER(S)	
Perry Chua	
ART DIRECTOR	
Thomas Billingsley Photographer	
CLIENT	
NOTES	
Die cut	

Westwerk Design
DESIGN FIRM | 001
SPECIMEN

Dan West
DESIGNER(S)

Dan West
ART DIRECTOR

Details Corporate Events
CLIENT

NOTES

Illustrator CS3; 160 lb. Chocolate

Rule29 Creative
DESIGN FIRM | 002
SPECIMEN

Josh Jensen
DESIGNER(S)

Justin Ahrens
ART DIRECTOR

DVDNow
CLIENT

NOTES

InDesign CS3

Oxide Design Co.
DESIGN FIRM | 003
SPECIMEN

Joe Sparano, Drew Davies
DESIGNER(S)

Drew Davies
ART DIRECTOR

Word Made Flesh
CLIENT

NOTES

InDesign CS3, Illustrator CS3; 30-pt. chipboard, Mactac
Metro

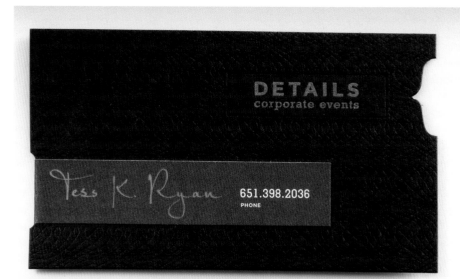

dvdnow™

XING CHEN VP - Engineering
xchen@dvdnowfreemovies.com

659 Executive Drive
Willowbrook, IL 60527

P 630 986 4422
F 630 325 5532

www.dvdnowfreemovies.com

002

word
MADE
flesh

Sarah Lance
Asia Regional
Coordinator,
Sari Bari Director

word MADE flesh — Jenna Christ Pashley, Field Advocate

word MADE flesh — Angelene Samuel, Project Coordinat

word MADE flesh — Erin Harrell, Field Administra

word MADE flesh — Christopher Heuertz, International Dire

word MADE flesh — Mandy Mow, Publications Edito

word MADE flesh — Hilary Wilken, Assistant to the Community Care Center

International Office

phileena.heuertz@
wordmadeflesh.org
P.O. Box 70
Omaha, NE 68101
USA

1.800.279.4543

003

pgm Design Associates

224 Wallace Avenue, Suite 409, Toronto, Ontario M6H 1V7 Canada
t 416 657 8881 f 416 352 5201 e aanderson@pgmdesign.ca

Andrew B. Anderson, Partner
OALA, CSLA, ASLA, IFLA

LANDSCAPE ARCHITECTURE

URBAN DESIGN

ENVIRONMENTAL PLANNING

001

002

003

Clear Space | *001*
DESIGN FIRM | SPECIMEN

Will Hum
DESIGNER(S)

Will Hum, Paul Ratchford
ART DIRECTOR

pgm Design Associates
CLIENT

NOTES

Illustrator CS3; Crane's Carnival Red

Creative Insight, LLC | *002*
DESIGN FIRM | SPECIMEN

Michael Lombardo
DESIGNER(S)

Michael Lombardo
ART DIRECTOR

Get Rooted
CLIENT

NOTES

Illustrator CS3; 100 lb. coated-varnish card stock

Another Limited Rebellion | *003*
DESIGN FIRM | SPECIMEN

Noah Scalin
ART DIRECTOR

Jason Guard
CLIENT

NOTES

Illustrator CS3; 100% postconsumer waste recycled paper

SWEETOUS BACKUS

- TWO SIDED
- OFTEN FULL BLEED
- PATTERNS OR IMAGES

- COLORFUL & ATTRACTIVE
- UNEXPECTEDLY EXPRESSIVE

KEY CHARACTERISTICS

The ancestors of *Cardious de Business* were commonly simple and distinctly conservative. As time passed, the need for a card to distinguish itself from the pack became increasingly important—a proverbial survival of the fittest. A certain species of cards—*Sweetous Backus*—rose to the occasion. They grew colorful, creative backsides to attract attention to themselves. Their numbers flourished as more and more of these creatures began to adopt similar practices. We have captured the best examples from the creative arms race to exhibit the most interesting two-sided creatures.

NOTES

design in motion

SMEE + BUSBY ARCHITECTS

J. Scott Busby, AIA
Principal
sbusby@smeebusby.com
www.smeebusby.com

29 Market Square #201
Knoxville, TN 37902
865.521.7550 voice
865.521.7551 fax

B

...CTOR

T 614.224.4535
F 614.224.4576
TROHRBACH@BASEARTCO.COM

ASE
ART CO

creating order from chaos

PRESCOTT PEREZ-FOX
brand development & design

prescott@perezfox.com

whatever it takes   whenever you call   wherever it takes us

KAUFMAN

Justin Tokos | V.P., Creative Director
justin@427design.com
www.427design.com

P. 330.535.0427 x 13 | **f.** 330.535.9427
190 N. Union St., Suite 200, Akron, Ohio 44304

...fman

24-HOUR EMERGENCY LINE
...roadcast.com

TEL 314. **421 2833**
PGR 888. **719 8433**
FAX 314. **421 2843**

HQ / BASE CAMP
1509 washington
avenue, suite **620**
saint louis, mo
63103
www.kaufmanbroadcast.com

the midwest leaders in live event broadcast

KAUFMAN BROADCAST

Fernando, CA

MATTHEW P. JOHNSON
Program Director

72 Log Cabin Road
Perkasie, PA 18944 USA
(c) 610.994.3814
(e) matt.johnson@ibecsolutions.org
www.ibecsolutions.org

Archrival	001
DESIGN FIRM	SPECIMEN
Joel Kreutzer	
DESIGNER(S)	
Clint Runge	
ART DIRECTOR	
W Hair Studio	
CLIENT	
NOTES	
Illustrator CS3	

tasteofinkstudios.com	002
DESIGN FIRM	SPECIMEN
Nathan Mummert	
DESIGNER(S)	
Nathan Mummert	
ART DIRECTOR	
Optimum Fotography	
CLIENT	
NOTES	
Photoshop; 14-pt. silk lamination, die cut	

The Designworks Group	003
DESIGN FIRM	SPECIMEN
Nate Salciccioli	
DESIGNER(S)	
IBEC	
CLIENT	

It's me, Donovan Newton Beery. Yes, these really are my business cards, and no, it doesn't matter if you read the whole thing as I nicely highlighted all of the important stuff. You're lucky I even typed this out rather than just writing out my number on a napkin, as my handwriting would most likely make it illegible. Well, at least you'd have an excuse for never calling then, saying my writing skills are well below par. That excuse is now void. You can reach me at area code 402 with the number 707-1119, or simply send a message via email to donovan@eleven19.com – either way, I should get the message. If you need to see samples of Eleven19's work, let us know and I'll put a brochure in the mail. If you want to be sneaky about it and look at our work without asking, just check out our website – it can be found at www.eleven19.com – but you probably already know that from seeing my email address. If you need to mail me anything, just use the mailing address listed on our website. I should probably also mention what all Eleven19 does, but if you were handed this card directly from me, you probably already know most of it. We look forward to speaking with you in the future, whether it be in 10 minutes, or a few years away. I really wanted the space of this entire card to be filled with text, so now I'm just writing stuff to make this side of the card look full. Most likely, you quit reading a while back, in fact, I even quit reading or proofing the text somewhere around the second sentence. Hope to hear from you soon. www.eleven19.com

001

Eleven19
DESIGN FIRM | 001 SPECIMEN

Donovan Beery
DESIGNER(S)

Donovan Beery
ART DIRECTOR

Eleven19
CLIENT

NOTES

InDesign CS3; Finch 80 lb. Cover

Louviere + Vanessa
DESIGN FIRM | 002 SPECIMEN

Jeff Louviere
DESIGNER(S)

Jeff Louviere
ART DIRECTOR

Jeff Louviere
CLIENT

NOTES

Illustrator CS3; Reclaimed elephant poop, Letterpress

WORKtoDATE
DESIGN FIRM | 003 SPECIMEN

Greg Bennett
DESIGNER(S)

Greg Bennett
ART DIRECTOR

WORKtoDATE
CLIENT

NOTES

Illustrator CS3, InDesign CS3; Printed 4-color front and back on Gmund Treasury paper

427 Design
DESIGN FIRM | 004 SPECIMEN

Allen Harrison
DESIGNER(S)

Justin Tokos
ART DIRECTOR

427 Design
CLIENT

NOTES

Photoshop CS3, Illustrator CS3, InDesign CS3; Letterpress on Chipboard

002

003

Justin Tokos | V.P., Creative Director
justin@427design.com
www.427design.com

p. 330.535.0427 x 13 | **f.** 330.535.9427
190 N. Union St., Suite 200, Akron, Ohio 44304

004

EMEDIA*Creative*
DESIGN TO GROW YOUR BUSINESS

kristie simpson reception busy bee

91 watkin street, newtown nsw 2042
p 2 9557 3366 **f** 2 9557 3700
e kristie@emediacreative.com.au
emediacreative.com.au

EMEDIA*Creative*
DESIGN TO GROW YOUR BUSINESS

001

*a circle of creative professionals
collaborating to grow your business*

VINE360

Joy Renée | Creative Director
50 N 4th Ave | #18B | Mpls MN 55401
Office 612 208 1911 | Cell 952 200 0794
www.VINE360.com | Joy@VINE360.com

002

p 847 702 5500   e nancy@nancyshouse.com

Nancy Goodman
nancyshouse.com

003

MICHAEL BROOK

MICHAEL BROOK
P H O T O G R A P H Y

27 ROBINWOOD AVENUE, UNIT 1
JAMAICA PLAIN, MA 02130

857.272.1385 | mdbrook@gmail.com
www.michaelbrookphotography.com

004

Emedia Creative	*001*
DESIGN FIRM	SPECIMEN
Jenni Cubis	
DESIGNER(S)	
Jenni Cubis	
ART DIRECTOR	
Emedia Creative	
CLIENT	
NOTES	
Illustrator CS3; White Knight with clear foil and varnish	

Joy Renee Design (formerly VINE360)	*002*
DESIGN FIRM	SPECIMEN
Joy Renee	
DESIGNER(S)	
Joy Renee Design (formerly VINE360)	
CLIENT	
NOTES	
Illustrator CS3, Photoshop CS3	

Grip Design	*003*
DESIGN FIRM	SPECIMEN
Josh Blaylock	
DESIGNER(S)	
Kelly Kaminski	
ART DIRECTOR	
Nancy Goodman	
CLIENT	
NOTES	
Illustrator CS3	

Roycroft Design	*004*
DESIGN FIRM	SPECIMEN
Jennifer Roycroft, Kaitlin Imwalle	
DESIGNER(S)	
Jennifer Roycroft	
ART DIRECTOR	
Michael Brook Photography	
CLIENT	
NOTES	
InDesign CS3; Mohawk Navajo	

Megan Cummins	001
DESIGN FIRM	SPECIMEN
Megan Cummins	
DESIGNER(S)	
Bare Cottyn	
CLIENT	
NOTES	
Illustrator CS3, Photoshop CS3	

Design Circus	002
DESIGN FIRM	SPECIMEN
Melissa Blasz	
DESIGNER(S)	
Melissa Blasz	
ART DIRECTOR	
Design Circus	
CLIENT	
NOTES	
InDesign CS3; Neenah Classic Columns, crack-and-peel label	

Zync Communications	003
DESIGN FIRM	SPECIMEN
Mike Kasperski, Peter C. Wong	
DESIGNER(S)	
Marko Zonta, Mike Kasperski	
ART DIRECTOR	
Blue Bamboo Yoga	
CLIENT	
NOTES	
Illustrator CS3, Photoshop CS3; Mohawk Navajo	

001

002

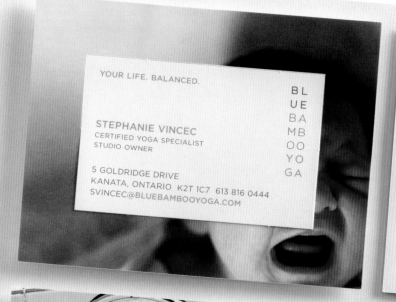

YOUR LIFE. BALANCED.

BL
UE
BA
MB
OO
YO
GA

STEPHANIE VINCEC
CERTIFIED YOGA SPECIALIST
STUDIO OWNER

5 GOLDRIDGE DRIVE
KANATA, ONTARIO K2T 1C7 613 816 0444
SVINCEC@BLUEBAMBOOYOGA.COM

KANATA LAKES
5 GOLDRIDGE DRIVE
KANATA, ON K2T 1C7
613 816 0444

BRIDLEWOOD
64 STONEHAVEN DRIVE
KANATA, ON K2M 2Y2
613 591 YOGA (9642)

INFO@BLUEBAMBOOYOGA.COM

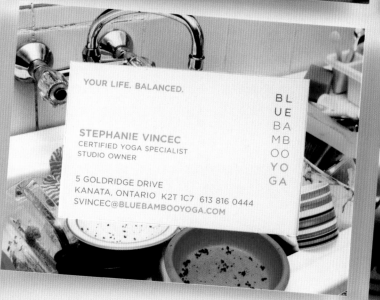

YOUR LIFE. BALANCED.

BL
UE
BA
MB
OO
YO
GA

STEPHANIE VINCEC
CERTIFIED YOGA SPECIALIST
STUDIO OWNER

5 GOLDRIDGE DRIVE
KANATA, ONTARIO K2T 1C7 613 816 0444
SVINCEC@BLUEBAMBOOYOGA.COM

YOUR LIFE. BALANCED.

BL
UE
BA
MB
OO
YO
GA

STEPHANIE VINCEC
CERTIFIED YOGA SPECIALIST
STUDIO OWNER

5 GOLDRIDGE DRIVE
KANATA, ONTARIO K2T 1C7 613 816 0444
SVINCEC@BLUEBAMBOOYOGA.COM

003

Jonathan Chubb
Graphic Designer

+44 (0)7717743644
hello@arkstudio.co.uk
www.arkstudio.co.uk

Ark
Little Trelabe
Bray Shop
Callington
Cornwall
PL17 8QL

paeonia
FLORAL

763 533 2554 phone
763 533 2488 fax

4150 west broadway ave
robbinsdale, mn 55422

paeoniafloral.com

002

kelly boyle
art director
cell: 203.558.1660
email: kelly@kboyle.com
website: www.kboyle.com

003

Louviere + Vanessa
DESIGN FIRM | 001 SPECIMEN

Jeff Louviere
DESIGNER(S)

Jeff Louviere
ART DIRECTOR

Heather Ferrell
CLIENT

NOTES
Illustrator CS3; chipboard, Letterpress

Maas Design
DESIGN FIRM | 002 SPECIMEN

Matthew Van Der Maas
DESIGNER(S)

Matthew Van Der Maas
ART DIRECTOR

Media Lounge Productions
CLIENT

NOTES
InDesign CS3; Utopia coated

Ten26 Design Group
DESIGN FIRM | 003 SPECIMEN

Kelly Demakis
DESIGNER(S)

Kelly Demakis
ART DIRECTOR

Ten26 Design Group - Custom invitations
CLIENT

NOTES
Illustrator CS3; Cover, Bright White Strathmore 88 lb.

001

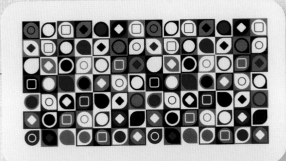

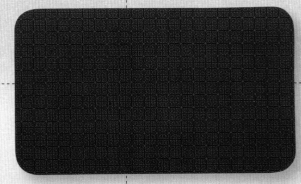

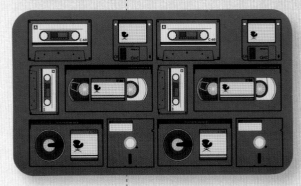

Media Lounge Productions
28826 John R.
Madison Heights, MI 48071
Office: 248.544.2707
Fax: 248.544.2772
Cell: 248.640.3788
matt@medialoungeproductions.com

MATT GREEN
CREATIVE DIRECTOR

 media lounge

COMMERCIAL VIDEO PRODUCTION · JINGLES & AUDIO · PRINT MEDIA · WEB DESIGN · GRAPHICS

002

ten26 design
CUSTOM INVITATIONS

kelly demakis

432 DIAMANDO STREET
CRYSTAL LAKE, ILLINOIS 60012
(CELL) 630-244-5741 (FAX) 815-280-0902
KELLY@TEN26CUSTOMINVITATIONS.COM
WWW.TEN26CUSTOMINVITATIONS.COM

003

001

002

David Dayco		001
DESIGN FIRM		SPECIMEN
David Dayco		
DESIGNER(S)		
David Dayco		
ART DIRECTOR		
Gopi Duillon, Makeup Artist		
CLIENT		
NOTES		
CS3; Classic Linen 120 lb. coated		

TOKY Branding + Design		002
DESIGN FIRM		SPECIMEN
Jamie Banks-George		
DESIGNER(S)		
Eric Thoelke		
ART DIRECTOR		
Kaufman Broadcast		
CLIENT		
NOTES		
Illustrator CS3; Mohawk Superfine Ultrawhite Smooth		

David Dayco		003
DESIGN FIRM		SPECIMEN
David Dayco		
DESIGNER(S)		
David Dayco		
ART DIRECTOR		
Katie Scott, Digital Artist		
CLIENT		
NOTES		
CS3; Neenah Environment 120 lb. coated		

003

Heather Mason Design | 001
DESIGN FIRM | SPECIMEN

Heather Mason
DESIGNER(S)

All Paws Dog Training
CLIENT

NOTES
Photoshop CS3, Illustrator CS3, InDesign CS3; 100 lb.
Cover, spot UV

TOKY Branding + Design | 002
DESIGN FIRM | SPECIMEN

Benjamin Franklin
DESIGNER(S)

Eric Thoelke
ART DIRECTOR

Appistry
CLIENT

NOTES
Creative Suite, Quark; Mohawk Superfine Ultrawhite

TOKY Branding + Design | 003
DESIGN FIRM | SPECIMEN

Geoff Story, Karin Soukup, Eric Thoelke
DESIGNER(S)

Eric Thoelke
ART DIRECTOR

S. King
CLIENT

NOTES
Illustrator CS3, Quark; Mohawk Superfine

TOKY Branding + Design | 004
DESIGN FIRM | SPECIMEN

Dan Klevorn
DESIGNER(S)

Eric Thoelke
ART DIRECTOR

Dotgray
CLIENT

NOTES
Illustrator CS3; Mohawk Superfine

Positive Modification Positive Results

Beth Madunic
Behaviorist/Trainer

414-881-3208
beth@allpawsdogtraining.net
www.allpawsdogtraining.net

ALL PAWS Dog Training, LLC.

001

The Fabric of Business™

Mark Minda
Sr. QA/CS Engineer
direct. 314 336 2837
cs pager. 314 253 2009
mark@appistry.com

One Cityplace Drive, Suite 470
St. Louis, MO 63141
main. 314 336 5080 **fax.** 314 336 5086

Appistry™

www.appistry.com

002

STACY F. KING
PRESIDENT AND CEO

IN-HOME COUTURE ACCESSORIES

ONE N. BRENTWOOD BLVD.
SUITE 510
ST. LOUIS MO 63105
T 314 657 1109 | F 314 657 1101
STACY@SKINGCOLLECTION.COM

SKINGCOLLECTION.COM

003

004

001

002

JEN MEYER
DIRECTOR OF MARKETING
JEN@STLRAC.ORG

6128 DELMAR BLVD
ST. LOUIS MO 63112

(314) 863 5811
(314) 863 6932 FAX
WWW.ART-STL.COM

REGIONAL ARTS
COMMISSION OF ST. LOUIS

003

Lady SKY★WRITER

Anne B. Kerr   anne@ladyskywriter.com
612-865-KERR (5377)

www.LadySkywriter.com
STORYTELLING: ONLINE

004

Square Feet Design	001
DESIGN FIRM	SPECIMEN
Marcella Kovac	
DESIGNER(S)	
Lauren Marwil	
ART DIRECTOR	
Bar 108	
CLIENT	
NOTES	
Illustrator CS3; Mohawk Superfine Ultrawhite 130 lb. Cover	

Firebelly Design	002
DESIGN FIRM	SPECIMEN
Will Miller, Sage Brown	
DESIGNER(S)	
Dawn Hancock	
ART DIRECTOR	
Arise Chicago	
CLIENT	
NOTES	
Creative Suite; Domtar Cougar Natural	

TOKY Branding + Design	003
DESIGN FIRM	SPECIMEN
Eric Thoelke, Jamie Banks-George	
DESIGNER(S)	
Eric Thoelke	
ART DIRECTOR	
Regional Arts Commission of St. Louis	
CLIENT	
NOTES	
Illustrator CS3; Mohawk Superfine Ultrawhite Smooth	

Adsoka	004
DESIGN FIRM	SPECIMEN
Gretchen Westbrock	
DESIGNER(S)	
Lady Skywriter	
CLIENT	
NOTES	
Illustrator CS3; Cougar 100 lb. Cover	

Greco Design	001
DESIGN FIRM	SPECIMEN

André Felipe (Tidé), Bruno Nunes
DESIGNER(S)

Gustavo Greco
ART DIRECTOR

Greco Design
CLIENT

NOTES

Illustrator CS3; Couché Matte 300 gsm laminate matte

TOKY Branding + Design	002
DESIGN FIRM	SPECIMEN

Katy Fischer, Simon Lam
DESIGNER(S)

Eric Thoelke
ART DIRECTOR

Butler's Boardroom
CLIENT

NOTES

Creative Suite; Mohawk Superfine Ultrawhite Eggshell

TOKY Branding + Design	003
DESIGN FIRM	SPECIMEN

Katy Fischer
DESIGNER(S)

Eric Thoelke
ART DIRECTOR

Butler's Pantry
CLIENT

NOTES

Creative Suite; Mohawk Superfine Ultrawhite Eggshell

ANDRÉ FELIPE (TIDÉ)
celular (31) 9631 9634
telefone (31) 3287 5835

Rua Rio Verde 150 Anchieta
cep 30.310-750 Belo Horizonte
tide@grecodesign.com.br
www.grecodesign.com.br

001

RICHARD L. NIX, JR.
PRESIDENT

BUTLER'S BOARDROOM

SIMPLY CATERING TO BUSINESS

5389 Arsenal Street, Saint Louis, Missouri 63139

PHONE 314/664.7681   FAX 314/664.9866

EMAIL rln@butlerspantry.com

BUTLERSBOARDROOM.COM

002

GREG ZIEGENFUSS
EXECUTIVE CHEF

BUTLER'S PANTRY

IN SERVICE SINCE 1966

5389 Arsenal Street, Saint Louis, Missouri 63139

PHONE 314/664.7680   FAX 314/664.9866

EMAIL greg@butlerspantry.com

BUTLERSPANTRY.COM

003

Erin Welch
Owner

815 E 65th Street
Indianapolis, IN 46220

317.306.9568

erin@8fifteen.com
www.8fifteen.com

001

002

003

Dan Sidor
1434 S. Logan St.
Denver, Co 80210
dan@dansidorphotography.com
303.722.0714

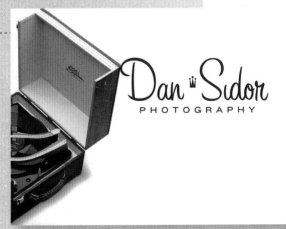

004

Timber Design Company Inc.	001
DESIGN FIRM	SPECIMEN
Lars Lawson	
ART DIRECTOR	
8Fifteen	
CLIENT	
NOTES	
Photoshop CS3, Illustrator Cs3; Crane Lettra Pearl White 110 lb.	

Firebelly Design	002
DESIGN FIRM	SPECIMEN
Will Miller	
DESIGNER(S)	
Dawn Hancock	
ART DIRECTOR	
Young Chicago Authors	
CLIENT	
NOTES	
Creative Suite; Domtar Cougar White	

FUNNEL: Eric Kass : Utilitarian + Commercial + Fine : Art	004
DESIGN FIRM	SPECIMEN
Eric Kass	
DESIGNER(S)	
John Bragg Photography	
CLIENT	
NOTES	
Illustrator CS3, Metallic gold offset litho, Black engraving, Label	

Honest Bros.	003
DESIGN FIRM	SPECIMEN
Eric Hines, Ryan Lee	
DESIGNER(S)	
Dan Sidor Photography	
CLIENT	
NOTES	
Illustrator CS3; Classic Crest	

FUNNEL: Eric Kass : Utilitarian +
Commercial + Fine : Art
DESIGN FIRM

001
SPECIMEN

Eric Kass
DESIGNER(S)

Forget Computers
CLIENT

NOTES
Illustrator CS3; Offset litho, gold engraving, blind
emboss, rubber stamp

Base Art Co.
DESIGN FIRM

002
SPECIMEN

Terry Rohrbach
DESIGNER(S)

Terry Rohrbach
ART DIRECTOR

Arccon Construction
CLIENT

NOTES
InDesign CS4; Navajo 100 lb. Cover

studiovertex
DESIGN FIRM

003
SPECIMEN

Michael Lindsay, Terry Liu
DESIGNER(S)

Michael Lindsay
ART DIRECTOR

studiovertex
CLIENT

NOTES
InDesign CS3; Cougar Opaque

FORGET COMPUTERS®

N° 312 602 5345
HELP@FORGETCOMPUTERS.COM

BEN GREINER

Chicago ILL.

001

ARCCON CONSTRUCTION

Jim Boggs Vice President
543 W. Rich Street, Columbus, Ohio 43215
Tel 614.298.0430 Fax 614.298.0429 Cell 614.402.0343
jboggs@arcconconstruction.com

www.arcconconstruction.com

002

STUDIOVERTEX HELPS BUSINESSES, NONPROFIT ORGANIZATIONS AND SOCIAL ENTREPRENEURS TO INNOVATE AND COMMUNICATE. WE WORK CLOSELY WITH YOU TO DEVELOP INTELLIGENT DESIGNS THAT PERSUADE, INFORM AND CLARIFY COMPLEX INFORMATION. TO LEARN MORE PLEASE CONTACT PRINCIPAL MICHAEL LINDSAY AT 206.838.7240.

studiovertex
108 S. WASHINGTON ST, SUITE 310
SEATTLE, WA 98104 USA
MICHAEL LINDSAY
206.838.7240
STUDIO-VERTEX.COM

THE
CREATIVEMETHOD.
STRATEGIC CREATIVE THINKERS

PIP HOPKINS
ACCOUNT MANAGER

E: PIP@THECREATIVEMETHOD.COM
WWW.THECREATIVEMETHOD.COM
STUDIO 10, 50 RESERVOIR STREET
SURRY HILLS NSW 2010 AUSTRALIA
P : +61 (0)2 8231 9977
F : +61 (0)2 8231 9980
M: +61 (0)411 566 114

WHERE
IDEAS
GROW

WHERE
IDEAS
GROW

WHERE
IDEAS
GROW

001

002

ruhrraum

sabine zimmermann
grafkdesignerin

cranger str. 15 a
44629 herne

0177.4213919
bine.zim@web.de

elfplusvier

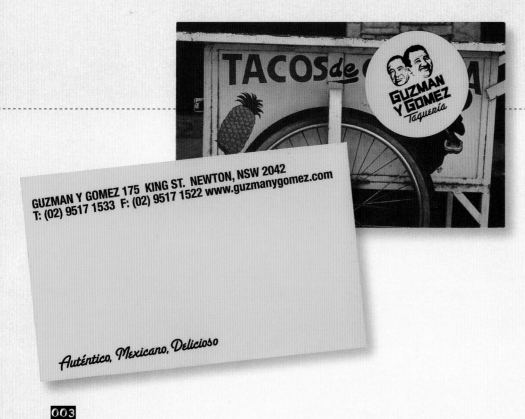

GUZMAN Y GOMEZ 175 KING ST. NEWTON, NSW 2042
T: (02) 9517 1533 F: (02) 9517 1522 www.guzmanygomez.com

Auténtico, Mexicano, Delicioso

003

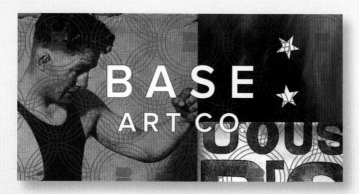

TERRY ROHRBACH
OWNER / CREATIVE DIRECTOR

17 BRICKEL ST, STE D   **T** 614.224.4535
COLUMBUS, OH 43215   **F** 614.224.4576
BASEARTCO.COM   TROHRBACH@BASEARTCO.COM

004

The Creative Method	001
DESIGN FIRM	SPECIMEN
Tony Ibbotson	
DESIGNER(S)	
Tony Ibbotson	
ART DIRECTOR	
The Creative Method	
CLIENT	
NOTES	
Illustrator CS3, Photoshop CS3; Specialty lenticular	

Sabine Zimmerman	002
DESIGN FIRM	SPECIMEN
Sabine Zimmerman	
DESIGNER(S)	
Sabine Zimmerman	
ART DIRECTOR	
Sabine Zimmerman	
CLIENT	
NOTES	
InDesign CS3; Zanders Medley Pure White	

The Creative Method	003
DESIGN FIRM	SPECIMEN
Tony Ibbotson	
DESIGNER(S)	
Tony Ibbotson	
ART DIRECTOR	
Guzman y Gomez	
CLIENT	
NOTES	
Photoshop CS3, Illustrator CS3; Knight Smooth 400 gsm from K.W. Doggett	

Base Art Co.	004
DESIGN FIRM	SPECIMEN
Terry Rohrbach	
DESIGNER(S)	
Terry Rohrbach	
ART DIRECTOR	
Base Art Co.	
CLIENT	
NOTES	
InDesign CS4; Navajo 100 lb. Cover, duplexed	

Sophy Sorim Lee
(917) 613-3598
growfloa@gmail.com

www.growfloa.com

001

Larry Ruvo

SENIOR MANAGING DIRECTOR

SOUTHERN WINE & SPIRITS
OF NEVADA

960 United Circle
Sparks, Nevada 89431-1585

Tel.775.355.4500
Fax.775.355.4509

002

003

:Baumann

STOFFE- UND TEXTILDISKONT

Baumann Stoffe- und Textildiskont
Gerbergasse 12 | A-5600 St. Johann/Pg.

T 0 64 12-43 87 | **F** 0 64 12-2 03 06 | **E** info@baumann-stoffe.at
I www.baumann-stoffe.at

Geschäftszeiten: Mo – Fr: 09:00 bis 17:00 Uhr

Betsy Ruhland
Floral Designer

THE
Florettes

THE
Florettes

PHONE 608 516 9508
EMAIL betsy@theflorettes.com
WEB theflorettes.com

004

Sophy (Sorim) Lee	001
DESIGN FIRM	SPECIMEN
Sophy (Sorim) Lee	
DESIGNER(S)	
NOTES	
Illustrator CS3, Photoshop CS3	

Mirko Ilić. Corp.	002
DESIGN FIRM	SPECIMEN
Mirko Ilić, Helen He	
DESIGNER(S)	
Mirko Ilić.	
ART DIRECTOR	
Southern Wines & Spirits of Nevada	
CLIENT	
NOTES	
Illustrator CS3	

Modelhart Design	003
DESIGN FIRM	SPECIMEN
Herbert O. Modelhart	
DESIGNER(S)	
Herbert O. Modelhart	
ART DIRECTOR	
Baumann Stoffe- und Textildiskont	
CLIENT	
NOTES	
Illustrator CS3, InDesign CS3; Olin 300 gsm	

Lefty Lexington Design	004
DESIGN FIRM	SPECIMEN
Nate Garn	
DESIGNER(S)	
Nate Garn	
ART DIRECTOR	
The Florettes	
CLIENT	
NOTES	
InDesign CS3, Illustrator CS3; Domtar	

Chen Design Associates | 001
DESIGN FIRM | SPECIMEN

Max Spector
DESIGNER(S)

Joshua Chen, Laurie Carrigan
ART DIRECTOR

Verve Coffee Roasters
CLIENT

NOTES

Illustrator CS3; Mohawk Superfine Ultrawhite Smooth
130 lb. Cover

Firebelly Design | 002
DESIGN FIRM | SPECIMEN

Will Miller
DESIGNER(S)

Dawn Hancock
ART DIRECTOR

The Queerist
CLIENT

NOTES

Creative Suite; French Muscletone Madero Beach

Pavone | 003
DESIGN FIRM | SPECIMEN

Robinson Smith
DESIGNER(S)

Robinson Smith
ART DIRECTOR

Harrisburg Shakespeare Festival
CLIENT

NOTES

Illustrator

001

002

003

Gabrielle DeNofrio, designer
717.571.1909. gabrielle.denofrio@gmail.com

Gabrielle DeNofrio, designer
717.571.1909. gabrielle.denofrio@gmail.com

001

002

003

TOKY Branding + Design	*001*
DESIGN FIRM	SPECIMEN
Katy Fischer, Jay David	
DESIGNER(S)	
Eric Thoelke	
ART DIRECTOR	
Baileys' Chocolate Bar	
CLIENT	
NOTES	
Creative Suite; 2-color	

Prescott Perez-Fox	*002*
DESIGN FIRM	SPECIMEN
Prescott Perez-Fox	
DESIGNER(S)	
Prescott Perez-Fox	
ART DIRECTOR	
Prescott Perez-Fox	
CLIENT	
NOTES	
InDesign CS3; 2-sided matte oaktag	

Counterform	*003*
DESIGN FIRM	SPECIMEN
Kurt Saberi	
DESIGNER(S)	
Kurt Saberi	
ART DIRECTOR	
The Canoe Group	
CLIENT	
NOTES	
Photoshop CS3, InDesign CS3	

Greco Design	*004*
DESIGN FIRM	SPECIMEN
Rafael Maia	
DESIGNER(S)	
Gustavo Greco	
ART DIRECTOR	
Corte & Cor	
CLIENT	
NOTES	
Illustrator CS3, Photoshop CS3; Couché Matte 300 gsm laminate matte, white spot UV varnish	

001

002

THE CANOE GROUP

David Frackelton, MS
Master Rower
david@thecanoegroup.com

4300 SW Parkview Avenue
Portland, Oregon 97225
503-708-2755 Mobile
TheCanoeGroup.com

THE CAN GRO

Deborah Elliott
Master Rower
deborah@thecano

4300 SW Parkview
Portland, Oregon 9
503-913-3716 Mob
TheCanoeGroup.cor

003

Eliani Paixão
Corte & Cor

Av. Francisco Deslandes 971 sl. 307
Anchieta Cep 30310 530
Belo Horizonte MG
Tel (31) 3287 7781
Cel (31) 9950 1636

004

Food + Editorial + Packaging Photography

Westwerk Design	001
DESIGN FIRM	SPECIMEN
Dan West	
DESIGNER(S)	
Dan West	
ART DIRECTOR	
Macemon Photography	
CLIENT	
NOTES	
Illustrator CS3	

macemon
photography

MARK MACEMON

E mark@macemonphoto.com   P 612 782 8272   W macemonphoto.com
A 681 17th Avenue NE Suite 400 Minneapolis Minnesota 55413

 001

Robin Easter Design	002
DESIGN FIRM	SPECIMEN
Jesse Wagner	
DESIGNER(S)	
Robin Easter Reeves	
ART DIRECTOR	
Smee + Busby Architects	
CLIENT	
NOTES	
Illustrator Cs3; Cougar White, thermography	

Studio Conover	003
DESIGN FIRM	SPECIMEN
Javier Leguizamo	
DESIGNER(S)	
David Conover	
ART DIRECTOR	
Metal Morphis	
CLIENT	
NOTES	
QuarkXPress; Classic Crest Natural White, embossing	

design in motion

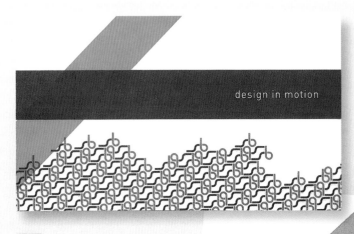

002

Evenson Design Group	004
DESIGN FIRM	SPECIMEN
Mark Sojka	
DESIGNER(S)	
Stan Evenson	
ART DIRECTOR	
Paddy Kean	
CLIENT	
NOTES	
Illustrator CS3; Classic Crest Avalanche Whites	

SMEE + BUSBY ARCHITECTS

J. Scott Busby, AIA
Principal
sbusby@smeebusby.com
www.smeebusby.com

29 Market Square #201
Knoxville, TN 37902
865.521.7550 voice
865.521.7551 fax

JEFF HEBETS
jeff@metalmorphis.com

METalMoRPhiS

602	840 0316	PHONE	4001	North 45th Street
	840 1279	FAX		Phoenix, Arizona 85018

WWW.METALMORPHIS.COM

003

KAULUA
HAWAIIAN CHOCOLATE COMPANY

Paddy Kean
CHOCOLATE MAKER

P.O. Box 682
Kilauea, HI 96754

808-828-6249 HOME
808-631-9443 MOBILE

kauluachocolate@me.com

004

The
GRAND TOUR

Furniture   Textiles   Objets d'Art

ffer

p. 480.990.8687 f. 480.990.1229

The Grand Tour
7134 E. Stetson Drive, Suite 100
Scottsdale, AZ 85251

info@thegrandtourhome.com
www.thegrandtourhome.com

001

pink blue black & orange co., ltd. (color party)
1128 rama 9 road, suanluang, bangkok 10250 thailand
tel. (662) 300 5124, fax. (662) 300 5123
mailus@colorparty.com, color_party@hotmail.com
www.colorparty.com
an associate of The Design Alliance™ a collaborative network
of asian design consultancies

pornchai run
print

rattanaporn puttanya
accountant

vichi
design dire

piyarat punuerai
graphic designer

002

STEVE SCOTT
GRAPHIC DESIGN

61 (0)424 386 715
STEVE@STEVESCOTTGRAPHICDESIGN.COM
STEVESCOTTGRAPHICDESIGN.COM

003

CHRISTINE ABERNATHY
2810 DAVENPORT ROAD
KNOXVILLE, TN 37920
TEL: 865.385.3413
www.happyyap.com

happy yap!
DOGGIE DAY CAMP

004

| Tomko Design | 001 |
| DESIGN FIRM | SPECIMEN |

Mike Tomko
DESIGNER(S)

Jennifer Bates, Mike Tomko
ART DIRECTOR

The Grand Tour
CLIENT

NOTES
Illustrator CS3; Topkote

| Pink Blue Black & Orange Co., Ltd. | 002 |
| DESIGN FIRM | SPECIMEN |

Manisa Lekprayoon, Perund Sethabutra
DESIGNER(S)

Vichean Tow
ART DIRECTOR

Pink Blue Black & Orange Co., Ltd.
CLIENT

NOTES
Illustrator CS3

| Steve Scott Graphic Design | 003 |
| DESIGN FIRM | SPECIMEN |

Steve Scott
DESIGNER(S)

Steve Scott
ART DIRECTOR

Steve Scott Graphic Design
CLIENT

NOTES
Illustrator CS3, InDesign CS3; 300 gsm silk matte laminated

| Robin Easter Design | 004 |
| DESIGN FIRM | SPECIMEN |

Amber Purdy
DESIGNER(S)

Robin Easter Reeves
ART DIRECTOR

Happy Yap! Doggie Day Camp
CLIENT

NOTES
Illustrator CS3

Cosmetologist
714.655.0441
hollypoole.cosmo@yahoo.com

CHERRYL MEURET, President
cherryl@coolatogelato.com

524 S GAY ST - KNOXVILLE, TN 37902
865.675.6060 - www.coolatogelato.com

003

STARK LEGAL
CONSULTING
Not just a law firm

S|L|C

Troy A. Stark, Esq.

(p) **(952) 960-5727**
(f) **(952) 960-8127**
(e) **tstark@stark-legal.com**

7701 France Avenue South, Suite 200 | Edina, MN 55435
www.stark-legal.com

004

Voicebox Creative	*001*
DESIGN FIRM	SPECIMEN
Voicebox Creative	
DESIGNER(S)	
Jacques Rossouw	
ART DIRECTOR	
Vintage Point	
CLIENT	
NOTES	
Illustrator CS3	

Two Twenty Two Creative	*002*
DESIGN FIRM	SPECIMEN
Lane Durante	
DESIGNER(S)	
Lane Durante	
ART DIRECTOR	
Holly Poole	
CLIENT	
NOTES	
Illustrator CS3	

Robin Easter Design	*003*
DESIGN FIRM	SPECIMEN
Travis Gray, Lauren Ray Wagner	
DESIGNER(S)	
Robin Easter Reeves	
ART DIRECTOR	
Coolato Gelato	
CLIENT	
NOTES	
Illustrator CS3; Cougar Natural 100 lb. Cover, thermography	

Adsoka	*004*
DESIGN FIRM	SPECIMEN
Kayla Stearns	
DESIGNER(S)	
Stark Legal Consulting	
CLIENT	
NOTES	
InDesign CS3; Cougar 100 lb. Cover	

001

DEAN ANDREWS
Director
dandrews@hsong.org

210 W. River Drive
St. Charles, IL 60174
P 630.377.0800 F 630.587.9696
www.hsong.org

HARRIETTE'S SONG

002

003

004

001

| FUNNEL: Eric Kass : Utilitarian +
Commercial + Fine : Art | 001 |
| DESIGN FIRM | SPECIMEN |

Eric Kass
DESIGNER(S)

Somersaults Life Archives
CLIENT

NOTES
Illustrator; Letterpress, Offset label

| FUNNEL: Eric Kass : Utilitarian +
Commercial + Fine : Art | 002 |
| DESIGN FIRM | SPECIMEN |

Eric Kass
DESIGNER(S)

The Goods Life
CLIENT

NOTES
Illustrator; Offset litho

| Tomato Kosir S.P. | 003 |
| DESIGN FIRM | SPECIMEN |

Tomato Kosir
DESIGNER(S)

Tomato Kosir
ART DIRECTOR

Draz Knitwork
CLIENT

NOTES
Illustrator CS3, Photoshop CS3; on 300 gsm offset

002

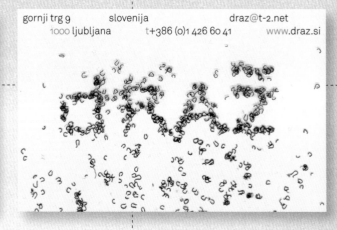

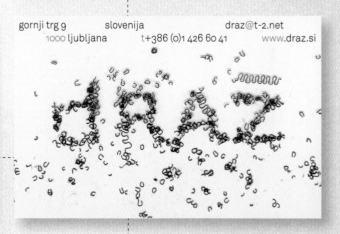

003

001

002

Alphabet Arm Design	001
DESIGN FIRM	SPECIMEN
Aaron Belyea, Ryan Frease, Chris Piascik, Ira F. Cummings	
DESIGNER(S)	
Aaron Belyea	
ART DIRECTOR	
Alphabet Arm Design	
CLIENT	
NOTES	
Creative Suite; Cougar Opaque arrow punch	

Insight Design Communications	002
DESIGN FIRM	SPECIMEN
Tracy Holderman	
DESIGNER(S)	
Tracy Holderman	
ART DIRECTOR	
Insight Design Communications	
CLIENT	
NOTES	
Thick paper with applied tape	

Brandhouse	003
DESIGN FIRM	SPECIMEN
Bronwen Edwards	
DESIGNER(S)	
David Beard	
ART DIRECTOR	
Alexa Cohen	
CLIENT	
NOTES	
Foil blocking	

alexa
Production Consultant

Alexa Cohen
12 Oliphant St
London W10 4EG
+44 (0)20 8969 1179
07785 511627
alexajcohen@yahoo.co.uk

your partner in crime

003

Grip Design
DESIGN FIRM | 001 SPECIMEN

Camay Ho, Josh Blaylock
DESIGNER(S)

Kelly Kaminski
ART DIRECTOR

Hooray Purée
CLIENT

NOTES
Illustrator CS3

Robin Easter Design
DESIGN FIRM | 002 SPECIMEN

Benjamin Finch
DESIGNER(S)

Robin Easter Reeves
ART DIRECTOR

Robin Easter Design
CLIENT

NOTES
Illustrator Cs3; Cougar Opaque, 130 lb. white Cover

airG
DESIGN FIRM | 003 SPECIMEN

Victoria Wong
DESIGNER(S)

Alan Woo
ART DIRECTOR

airG
CLIENT

NOTES
Photoshop CS3, Illustrator CS3, InDesign CS3

airG

1155 Robson St. Suite #706
Vancouver, BC Canada V6E 1B5
T: +1.604.408.2228
F: +1.866.874.8136

www.airG.com

001

003

Kristine Smith
Co-Founder / Artistic Director

12-A Jules Lane
New Brunswick, NJ 08901

T 732 247 2295
F 732 247 2344
ksmith@InSpiraArts.com
InSpiraArts.com

004

InSpira Performing Arts & Cultural Center

FUNNEL: Eric Kass : Utilitarian +	
Commercial + Fine : Art	*001*
DESIGN FIRM	SPECIMEN
Eric Kass	
DESIGNER(S)	
Mary Kate McKenna Photography	
CLIENT	
NOTES	
Illustrator CS3; Offset litho, satin laminate	

Airside	*002*
DESIGN FIRM	SPECIMEN
Airside	
DESIGNER(S)	
Airside	
ART DIRECTOR	
Airside	
CLIENT	
NOTES	
Illustrator CS3	

Claudia Dionne	*003*
DESIGN FIRM	SPECIMEN
Claudia Dionne	
DESIGNER(S)	
Claudia Dionne	
ART DIRECTOR	
Ishi, Regina Barrios jewel designer	
CLIENT	
NOTES	
Photoshop CS3; Reused cardboard, printed stamps	

3rd Edge Communications	*004*
DESIGN FIRM	SPECIMEN
Nick Schmitz	
DESIGNER(S)	
Frankie Gonzalez	
ART DIRECTOR	
InSpira Performing Arts & Cultural Center	
CLIENT	

001

TDC
ST. LOUIS SM

TDC ST. LOUIS

DAVID SHERMAN, III
PRESIDENT

190 Carondelet Plaza, Suite 1450 St. Louis, MO 63105
P: 314-880-9999 F: 314-880-9997 M: 314-378-1405
E: dsherman@tdcstl.com www.tdcstl.com

Securities offered through LPL Financial Member FINRA/SIPC

KNOWLEDGE OF WEALTH ‖ WEALTH OF KNOWLEDGE

002

W. Scott McKenna
Sr. Development Project Manager
The Simpson Organization

701 E. Bay Street Suite 300
Charleston, SC 29403
T| 843.576.4084 C| 843.270.7878
F| 843.576.4086
wsmsimpson@earthlink.net
Scott@CigarFactoryCharleston.com

THE LAUREL™
AT MERCANTILE EXCHANGE

LUXURY CONDOS

JAY HEDERMAN
SALES MANAGER

625 WASHINGTON AVE., ST. LOUIS, MISSOURI 63101
P: 314-241-3900 F: 314-241-3901 M: 314-814-9830
E: jay@thelaurelstlouis.com W: www.thelaurelstlouis.com

003

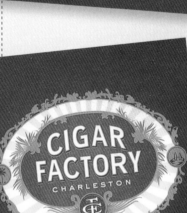

CIGAR
FACTORY
CHARLESTON

004

BUNDANONTRUST

001

DEBORAH ELY

Chief Executive Officer
T +61 2 4422 2100
F +61 2 4422 7190
deborah@bundanon.com.au

BUNDANON TRUST
PO Box 3343
North Nowra NSW 2541 Australia
bundanon.com.au

Bob Rains
EL PRESIDENTE

bob@letsmakeitawesome.com
CEL 617.319.4231
TEL 781.740.4490
350 Lincoln Street, Suite 2215
Hingham, MA 02043
LMIA Inc.

LetsMakeItAwesome.com

LetsMakeItAwesome.com

002

003

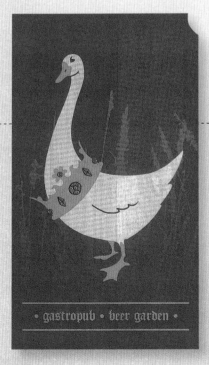

004

Boccalatte	001
DESIGN FIRM	SPECIMEN
Suzanne Boccalatte	
DESIGNER(S)	
Suzanne Boccalatte	
ART DIRECTOR	
Bundanon Trust	
CLIENT	
NOTES	
InDesign CS3; Knight Smooth 120 gsm	

Alphabet Arm Design	002
DESIGN FIRM	SPECIMEN
Ryan Frease	
DESIGNER(S)	
Aaron Belyea	
ART DIRECTOR	
Bob Rains	
CLIENT	
NOTES	
Creative Suite; Silver foil stamp	

tasteofinkstudios.com	003
DESIGN FIRM	SPECIMEN
Nathan Mummert	
DESIGNER(S)	
Nathan Mummert	
ART DIRECTOR	
Casino Tesoro	
CLIENT	
NOTES	
Photoshop CS3; 15 pt. silk lamination, spot varnish, silver foil	

Robin Easter Design	004
DESIGN FIRM	SPECIMEN
Amber Purdy, Benjamin Finch	
DESIGNER(S)	
Robin Easter Reeves	
ART DIRECTOR	
The Crown & Goose	
CLIENT	
NOTES	
Illustrator Cs3; Classic Crest Natural 130 lb. Cover	

INTERACTIVOUS CARDIOUS

- THREE-DIMENSIONAL
- FEATURE UNIQUE ELEMENTS
- HIGHLY TACTILE
- INCLUDES FOLDS OR BENDS
- ENCOURAGES EXPLORATION

KEY CHARACTERISTICS

Every creature in the *Cardious de Business* kingdom interacts with humans as well as other specimens. However, a specific genus of cards has found new and innovative ways of sharing their messages with the world. Excellent examples of *Interactivous Cardious* have been found in all corners of the world. Some are die-cut or embossed to highlight their most vital features. Others stake their claim into three-dimensional space by growing folds and bends; while others are transparent or translucent to get noticed. Regardless, these creatures are highly evolved and quite extravagant in their efforts. The following pages feature a variety of examples of this fast-growing and distinctly engaging genus.

NOTES

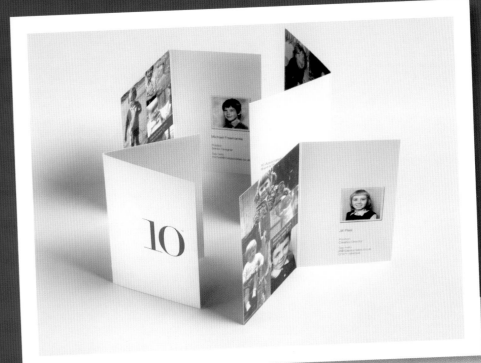

Hi re me.

scratch here for the answer to life. Please note: resulting joy may prove overwhelming.

Hi

scratch here for the answer to life. Please note: resulting joy may prove overwhelming.

Megan Cummins

graphic designer www.megancummins.com call 901.485.9428 e-mail cumminsdesign@gmail.com

aj andrade   ass kicker
aj@tmarksdesign.com

803 south king street seattle, wash. 98104
206 628.6427   206 628.6428 fax
tmarksdesign.com

002

003

tmarks design	001
DESIGN FIRM	SPECIMEN
Terry Marks	
DESIGNER(S)	
Terry Marks	
ART DIRECTOR	
tmarks design	
CLIENT	
NOTES	
Freehand; Stardream, Bronze sewn	

Third Sector Creative	002
DESIGN FIRM	SPECIMEN
Catherine Brautigan	
DESIGNER(S)	
Linsey Sieger	
ART DIRECTOR	
Vince Bruce, The Wizard of Whips & Ropes	
CLIENT	
NOTES	
InDesign CS3, Photoshop CS3	

Sophy (Sorim) Lee	003
DESIGN FIRM	SPECIMEN
Sophy (Sorim) Lee	
DESIGNER(S)	
NOTES	
Photoshop Cs3; Cardboard	

| AEN | 001 |
| DESIGN FIRM | SPECIMEN |

Aen Tan
DESIGNER(S)

Aen Tan
ART DIRECTOR

Aen Tan
CLIENT

NOTES

Illustrator CS3; PolyFrost plastic

| Ó! | 002 |
| DESIGN FIRM | SPECIMEN |

Einar Gylfason
DESIGNER(S)

Einar Gylfason
ART DIRECTOR

1"
CLIENT

NOTES

Illustrator CS3; 1.2 mm Absorbent paper

| Intrinsic Design | 003 |
| DESIGN FIRM | SPECIMEN |

Linda Winsbro, Patti Barrett
DESIGNER(S)

Intrinsic Design
CLIENT

NOTES

InDesign CS3, Illustrator CS3; Mohawk Beckett Cambric
100 lb. coated

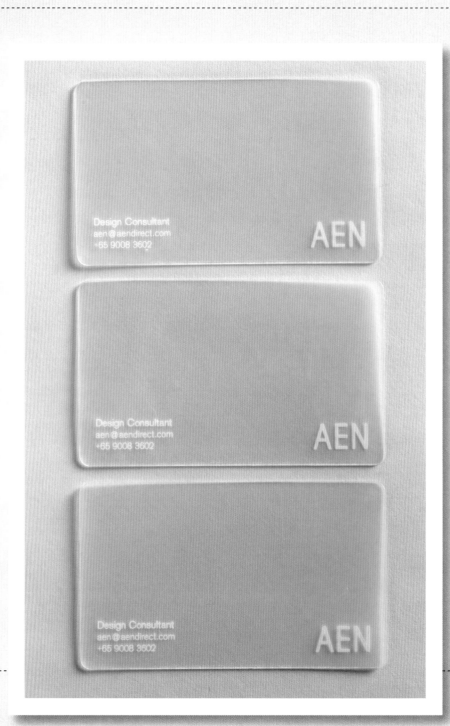

001

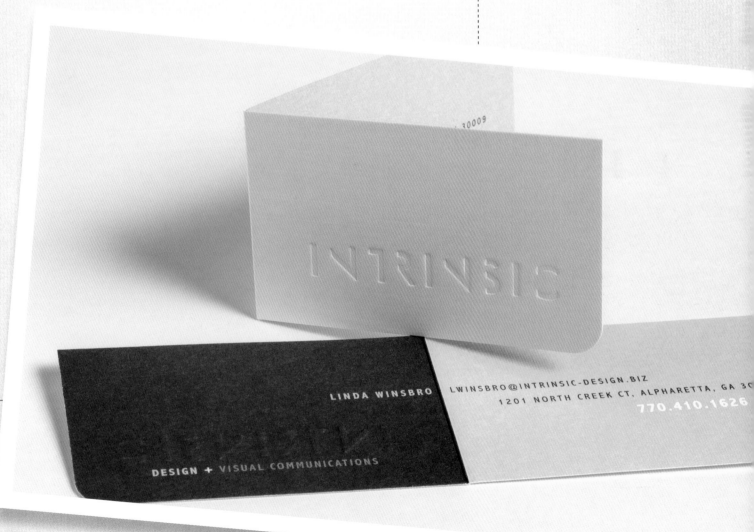

002

003

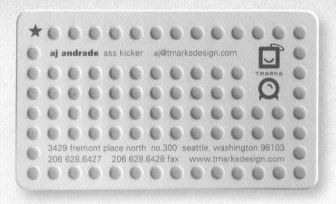

001

002

003

tmarks design	001
DESIGN FIRM	SPECIMEN
Terry Marks	
DESIGNER(S)	
Terry Marks	
ART DIRECTOR	
tmarks design	
CLIENT	
NOTES	

Freehand; Mohawk Superfine Ultrawhite 100 lb. coated

tmarks design	002
DESIGN FIRM	SPECIMEN
Terry Marks	
DESIGNER(S)	
Terry Marks	
ART DIRECTOR	
tmarks design	
CLIENT	
NOTES	

Freehand; Mohawk Superfine Smooth Ultrawhite
Cover 160 lb.

Garden Variety Designs	003
DESIGN FIRM	SPECIMEN
Meridith Byrne-Paulhus	
DESIGNER(S)	
Jonathan L. Smith	
ART DIRECTOR	
Kristen O'Malley	
CLIENT	
NOTES	

Illustrator CS3; Crane Signature in Espresso, fused with
Fox River crushed leaf in lavender sparkles

Faust
DESIGN FIRM | *001*
SPECIMEN

Bob Faust
DESIGNER(S)

Bob Faust
ART DIRECTOR

Bryan Zises
CLIENT

NOTES
InDesign CS3; French Frostone 70 lb., text, Tundra

TOKY Branding + Design
DESIGN FIRM | *002*
SPECIMEN

Jay David, Jon Arnett
DESIGNER(S)

Eric Thoelke
ART DIRECTOR

TOKY Branding + Design
CLIENT

NOTES
Illustrator CS3; Printed on plastic

001

001

002

003

004

FUNNEL: Eric Kass : Utilitarian + Commercial + Fine : Art	*001*
DESIGN FIRM	SPECIMEN
Eric Kass	
DESIGNER(S)	
Films by Francesco	
CLIENT	
NOTES	
Illustrator CS3; Offset litho, black engraving	

Lloyds Graphic Design Ltd.	*002*
DESIGN FIRM	SPECIMEN
Alexander Lloyd	
DESIGNER(S)	
Alexander Lloyd	
ART DIRECTOR	
Rapaura Springs	
CLIENT	
NOTES	
Freehand MX; Matte art board 250 gsm	

10 Associates	*003*
DESIGN FIRM	SPECIMEN
Michael Freemantle	
DESIGNER(S)	
Jill Peel	
ART DIRECTOR	
10 Associates	
CLIENT	
NOTES	
Illustrator CS3; Skye Natural White, 2 colors, embossed.	

Paige Weber	*004*
DESIGN FIRM	SPECIMEN
Paige Weber	
DESIGNER(S)	
Paige Weber	
CLIENT	
NOTES	
Illustrator CS3	

Zande + Newman Design	001
DESIGN FIRM	SPECIMEN
Adam Newman	
DESIGNER(S)	
Twisted Fiction	
CLIENT	
NOTES	
InDesign CS3; Crane's Crest 100 lb.	

Z2 Marketing	002
DESIGN FIRM	SPECIMEN
Justin Ninneman	
DESIGNER(S)	
Justin Ninneman	
ART DIRECTOR	
Port City Studio	
CLIENT	
NOTES	
Quark, Illustrator CS3; Finch Fine Double Thick 100 lb. Cover, perforated, stapled, 2 colors	

squarehand.com	003
DESIGN FIRM	SPECIMEN
Monica Torrejón Kelly	
DESIGNER(S)	
Monica Torrejón Kelly	
ART DIRECTOR	
Squarehand	
CLIENT	
NOTES	
Illustrator CS3; Couché Plastified Matte, spot varnish	

FUNNEL: Eric Kass : Utilitarian + Commercial + Fine : Art	004
DESIGN FIRM	SPECIMEN
Eric Kass	
DESIGNER(S)	
Ed McCulloch Photo	
CLIENT	
NOTES	
Illustrator CS3; Letterpress, silkscreen envelope, stitched patch	

001

002

003

004

001

002

LARS LAWSON

PRINCIPAL

4402 NORTH COLLEGE AVE
INDIANAPOLIS, INDIANA
46205

P 317.921.0948
C 317.213.8509

LARS@TIMBERDESIGNCO.COM
TIMBERDESIGNCO.COM

003

theCIRCLESTUDIO.com
220 Julia Street
New Orleans, LA 70130

oibutscircle

SHANNON DOWNEY
shannon@thecirclestudio.com
T 504.322.7718 M 504.909.2355

004

Pascale Payant Design	001
DESIGN FIRM	SPECIMEN
Pascale Payant	
DESIGNER(S)	
Pascale Payant	
ART DIRECTOR	
Rénovations Bigras	
CLIENT	
NOTES	
Illustrator CS3; Sandpaper	

Robert Meyers Design	002
DESIGN FIRM	SPECIMEN
Robert Meyers	
DESIGNER(S)	
Robert Meyers Design	
ART DIRECTOR	
NOTES	
Cougar	

Timber Design Company	003
DESIGN FIRM	SPECIMEN
Lars Lawson	
ART DIRECTOR	
Timber Design Company	
CLIENT	
NOTES	
Freehand; Wood laminate, decals	

Zande + Newman Design	004
DESIGN FIRM	SPECIMEN
Loren Stephens	
DESIGNER(S)	
Adam Newman	
ART DIRECTOR	
Circle Studio	
CLIENT	
NOTES	
InDesign CS3; Crane's 110 lb. Cover	

| Rutka Weadock Design | 001 |
| DESIGN FIRM | SPECIMEN |

Darina Geiling
DESIGNER(S)

Anthony Rutka
ART DIRECTOR

Rutka Weadock Design
CLIENT

NOTES
QuarkXPress; Tagboard

| Andrea Gervasoni Visual Communication | 002 |
| DESIGN FIRM | SPECIMEN |

Andrea Gervasoni
DESIGNER(S)

Andrea Gervasoni
ART DIRECTOR

SkyRec Company Group
CLIENT

NOTES
InDesign CS3; Arjo Wiggins: Concept, Iridescent

| Boom Island | 003 |
| DESIGN FIRM | SPECIMEN |

Jim Jackson, Jeff Schweigert
ART DIRECTOR

Boom Island
CLIENT

NOTES
Illustrator CS3; Plastic

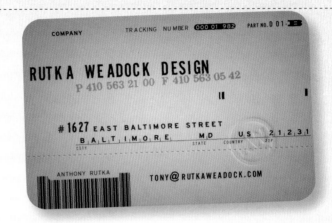

001

002

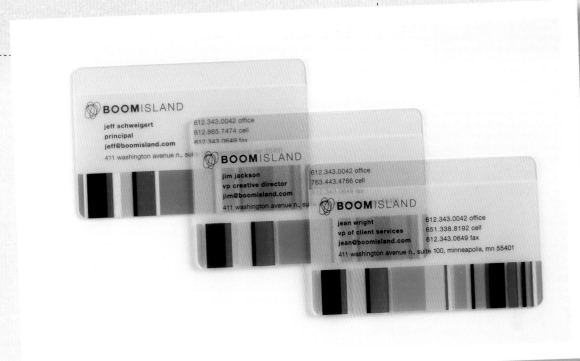

001

this is my **card**™

I am the creative director

MINE™ 190 Putnam St. San Francisco, CA 94110 415 647 6463 minesf.com

CHRISTOPHER SIMMO
cchs@minesf.com

002

003

004

Object 9	001
DESIGN FIRM	SPECIMEN
Object 9	
CLIENT	
NOTES	
Illustrator CS3, Photoshop CS3; Domed emboss, foil stamp	

MINE	002
DESIGN FIRM	SPECIMEN
Christopher Simmons, Tim Belonax	
DESIGNER(S)	
Christopher Simmons	
ART DIRECTOR	
MINE	
CLIENT	
NOTES	
Illustrator CS3; Two sheets 70 lb. Mohawk Options, laminated to Pegasus Midnight Black 80 lb. coated vellum	

Willoughby Design	003
DESIGN FIRM	SPECIMEN
Jessica McEntire	
DESIGNER(S)	
Ann Willoughby, Nate Hardin	
ART DIRECTOR	
Kevin Carroll	
CLIENT	
NOTES	
Creative Suite; Letterpress	

Extra Credit Projects	004
DESIGN FIRM	SPECIMEN
Nolan Abney	
DESIGNER(S)	
Rob Jackson	
ART DIRECTOR	
Extra Credit Projects	
CLIENT	
NOTES	
French Muscle Tone	

squarehand.com
DESIGN FIRM

001
SPECIMEN

Monica Torrejón Kelly
DESIGNER(S)

Monica Torrejón Kelly
ART DIRECTOR

The Buddy Project Recording Studio
CLIENT

NOTES

Illustrator Cs3; Couche Plastified Matte, spot varnish

Royal Fly LLP
DESIGN FIRM

002
SPECIMEN

Eunice Wee
DESIGNER(S)

Fabian Lim, Ken Tan
ART DIRECTOR

Royal Fly
CLIENT

NOTES

Illustrator CS3; 230 Artcard, matte lamination, deboss

MDG
DESIGN FIRM

003
SPECIMEN

Kris Greene
DESIGNER(S)

Tim Merry
ART DIRECTOR

Clausen and Company
CLIENT

NOTES

Illustrator CS3, InDesign CS3; Neenah Classic
Crest Cover

Scott Adams Design Associates
DESIGN FIRM

004
SPECIMEN

Scott Adams
ART DIRECTOR

Scott Adams Design Associates
CLIENT

NOTES

QuarkXPress

001

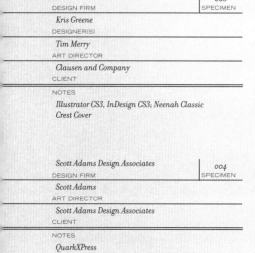

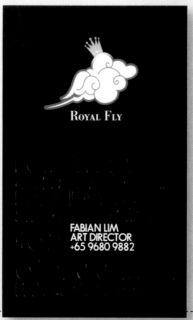

002

MARK CLAUSEN, CPA, MST
President

71 Turnpike Road
Southborough, Massachusetts 01745
mark@clausencompany.com
www.clausencompany.com

T : (508) 787 0008
F : (508) 787 0055

CLAUSEN AND CO.

CERTIFIED PUBLIC ACCOUNTANTS, PC · MAKING CENTS OF IT ALL

003

004

001

002

003

Creative Suitcase	001
DESIGN FIRM	SPECIMEN
Jennifer Wright	
DESIGNER(S)	
Rachel Clemens	
ART DIRECTOR	
Adlucent	
CLIENT	
NOTES	
Illustrator CS3; Manadnock and Neenah Soft Touch	

Clear Space	002
DESIGN FIRM	SPECIMEN
Will Hum	
DESIGNER(S)	
Will Hum, Paul Ratchford	
ART DIRECTOR	
Clear Space	
CLIENT	
NOTES	
Illustrator CS3; Classic Crest, Benefit Blue Yonder	

Clear Space	003
DESIGN FIRM	SPECIMEN
Will Hum	
DESIGNER(S)	
Will Hum	
ART DIRECTOR	
Del Monte Group	
CLIENT	
NOTES	
Illustrator CS3; Gilbert Oxford Cream, Gilbert Oxford Fired	

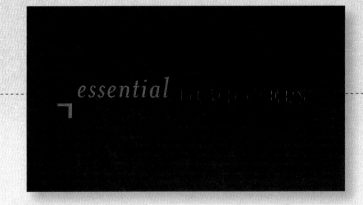

Miriello Grafico	001
DESIGN FIRM	SPECIMEN
Tracy Meiners	
DESIGNER(S)	
Ron Miriello	
ART DIRECTOR	
Eplica / Essential Discovery	
CLIENT	
NOTES	
Illustrator CS3; Strathmore	

001

essentialdiscovery.net

Daniel L. Sweeney, Esq.
NATIONAL DIRECTOR OF OPERATIONS

530 Davis Street, San Francisco, CA 94111

cell 619.787.3214 *free* 800.540.8792

dls@essentialdiscovery.net

Chen Design Associates	002
DESIGN FIRM	SPECIMEN
Max Spector, Shadi Kashefi	
DESIGNER(S)	
Joshua Chen	
ART DIRECTOR	
Stanford Lively Arts	
CLIENT	
NOTES	
InDesign CS3; Neenah Classic Columns Red Pepper, Solar White 120 lb. Cover	

visure	003
DESIGN FIRM	SPECIMEN
Nicole Cox, Carolina Aviles, Lorraine Albert	
DESIGNER(S)	
Nicole Cox	
ART DIRECTOR	
visure	
CLIENT	
NOTES	
InDesign CS3, Illustrator CS3, Freehand; Rives Design	

STANFORD LIVELY ARTS

http://livelyarts.stanford.edu

Extra Credit Projects	004
DESIGN FIRM	SPECIMEN
Nolan Abney	
DESIGNER(S)	
Rob Jackson	
ART DIRECTOR	
Extra Credit Projects	
CLIENT	

STANFORD
LIVELY ARTS

MICHELLE NICOLE LEE
DIRECTOR OF CAMPUS ENGAGEMENT

Stanford University
537 Lomita Mall, MC 2250
Stanford, CA 94305-2250

E   mnlee@stanford.edu

P   650-725-8938
F   650-723-8231
C   650-862-4064

002

christiansen : creative

eating, sleeping & breathing
graphic design. it's true.

Tricia Christiansen **creative director**

tricia@christiansencreative.com
715 381 8480

001

dailygrommet.com

DAILY GROMMET

Jules Pieri · Chief Executive Officer
jules@dailygrommet.com

o {877} 862-0222
m {781} 248-3099

002

003

004

christiansen : creative
DESIGN FIRM | 001 SPECIMEN

Tricia Christiansen
DESIGNER(S)

Tricia Christiansen
ART DIRECTOR

christiansen : creative
CLIENT

NOTES
InDesign CS3; Embossed, die cut, with sticker

Alphabet Arm Design | 002 SPECIMEN
DESIGN FIRM

Ira F. Cummings
DESIGNER(S)

Aaron Belyea
ART DIRECTOR

Jules Pieri
CLIENT

NOTES
Creative Suite; Letterpress; chipboard with paper label

Spark! Communications | 003 SPECIMEN
DESIGN FIRM

Sherri Lawton
DESIGNER(S)

Sherri Lawton
ART DIRECTOR

The John Christian Company
CLIENT

NOTES
Illustrator CS3; Chipboard, foil stamp, and embossing

Evenson Design Group | 004 SPECIMEN
DESIGN FIRM

Nicole Splatter, Dallas Duncan
DESIGNER(S)

Stan Evenson, Mark Sojka
ART DIRECTOR

Vinotéque
CLIENT

NOTES
Illustrator CS3; Neenah Environment Cover Ultra Bright
White 100 lb.

001

002

003

004

St. Bernadine Mission
Communications, Inc. | 001
DESIGN FIRM | SPECIMEN

Jennifer Hicks
DESIGNER(S)

Andrew Samuel
ART DIRECTOR

The Dog & Hydrant
CLIENT

NOTES
Illustrator CS3; Metal dog tag, stickers

designlab, inc | 002
DESIGN FIRM | SPECIMEN

Scott Gericke
DESIGNER(S)

Laura Burns Gericke
ART DIRECTOR

designlab, inc
CLIENT

NOTES
InDesign CS3, Illustrator CS3; Mohawk Superfine
Ultrawhite, 130 lb. Cover, eggshell finish

A3 Design | 003
DESIGN FIRM | SPECIMEN

Alan Altman
DESIGNER(S)

Amanda Altman
ART DIRECTOR

carbonhouse
CLIENT

NOTES
Illustrator CS3; 2x thick Classic Crest 130 lb.

Voicebox Creative | 004
DESIGN FIRM | SPECIMEN

Voicebox Creative
DESIGNER(S)

Jacques Rossouw
ART DIRECTOR

Sbragia Family Vineyards
CLIENT

NOTES
Illustrator CS3

Westwerk Design	001
DESIGN FIRM	SPECIMEN
Dan West	
DESIGNER(S)	
Dan West	
ART DIRECTOR	
Jaime Wickard	
CLIENT	
NOTES	
Illustrator CS3; Black card stock	

Clayton Junior	002
DESIGN FIRM	SPECIMEN
Clayton Junior	
DESIGNER(S)	
Clayton Junior	
ART DIRECTOR	
Clayton Junior	
CLIENT	
NOTES	
Hahnemühle Scraps	

Greco Design	003
DESIGN FIRM	SPECIMEN
Guilherme Woll, Sidney Telles	
DESIGNER(S)	
Gustavo Greco	
ART DIRECTOR	
Marcus Vieira	
CLIENT	
NOTES	
Illustrator, CS3; Couché Matte 300 gsm laminate matte with embossing.	

Oxide Design Co.	004
DESIGN FIRM	SPECIMEN
Drew Davies, Joe Sparano, Adam Torpin	
DESIGNER(S)	
Drew Davies	
ART DIRECTOR	
Oxide Design Co.	
CLIENT	
NOTES	
InDesign CS3, Illustrator CS3; Crane Lettra	

001

002

MARCUS VIEIRA
cel (11) 8314 9898
cel (31) 9983 7098
markuelo@yahoo.com.br

MARCUS VIEIRA
Rua Haddock Lobo 1175 apto11
Cerqueira César 014 14 003
São Paulo SP Brasil
markuelo@yahoo.com.br
tel (11) 3062 4498
cel (11) 8314 9898
cel (31) 9983 7098

003

Joe Sparano   Oxide Design Co.
COMMUNICATIONS AND INFORMATION DESIGN

3916 Farnam Street
Omaha, Nebraska 68131

(402) 344-0168
drew@oxidedesign.com

004

001

002

003

004

Firebelly Design	001
DESIGN FIRM	SPECIMEN
Will Miller	
DESIGNER(S)	
Dawn Hancock	
ART DIRECTOR	
Firebelly Foundation	
CLIENT	
NOTES	
Creative Suite; French Frostone Glacier	

Spring	002
DESIGN FIRM	SPECIMEN
Perry Chua	
DESIGNER(S)	
Perry Chua	
ART DIRECTOR	
Select Wines	
CLIENT	
NOTES	
Cork adhered to back of card, thermography logo	

Struck	003
DESIGN FIRM	SPECIMEN
Rich Black	
DESIGNER(S)	
Brandon Knowlden	
ART DIRECTOR	
Lush Lawn and Property Management	
CLIENT	
NOTES	
Illustrator CS3; 80 lb. postconsumer text	

Artista Muvek	004
DESIGN FIRM	SPECIMEN
Tamas Seres	
ART DIRECTOR	
Artista Muvek	
CLIENT	
NOTES	
InDesign CS3, Illustrator CS3; Rives Tradition, brown paper	

Spring	001
DESIGN FIRM	SPECIMEN
Perry Chua	
DESIGNER(S)	
Perry Chua	
ART DIRECTOR	
Spring Advertising	
CLIENT	

Type G	002
DESIGN FIRM	SPECIMEN
Mike Nelson	
DESIGNER(S)	
Mike Nelson	
ART DIRECTOR	
Solomon + Ferguson	
CLIENT	
NOTES	
Illustrator CS3; Mohawk Via, embossing and clear foil	

Reactor	003
DESIGN FIRM	SPECIMEN
Chase Wilson	
DESIGNER(S)	
Clifton Alexander	
ART DIRECTOR	
Reactor — Creator of Epic Brands	
CLIENT	

001

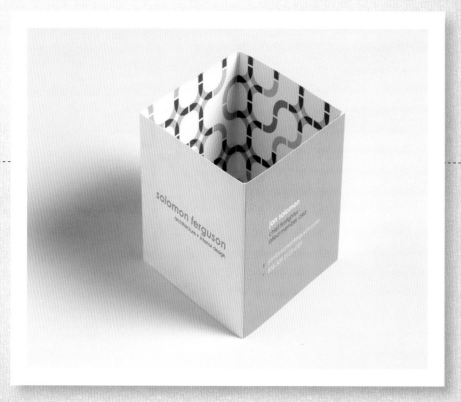

002

003

white_space	*001*
DESIGN FIRM	SPECIMEN
Mark Masterson	
DESIGNER(S)	
Mark Masterson	
ART DIRECTOR	
901 Tequila	
CLIENT	
NOTES	
Illustrator CS3; Reich Shine	

Megan Cummins	*002*
DESIGN FIRM	SPECIMEN
Megan Cummins	
DESIGNER(S)	
Megan Cummins	
ART DIRECTOR	
Megan Cummins	
CLIENT	
NOTES	
Illustrator CS3; Classic Crest 130 lb., foil stamp	

Organic Grid	*003*
DESIGN FIRM	SPECIMEN
Michael McDonald	
ART DIRECTOR	
Organic Grid	
CLIENT	
NOTES	
Illustrator CS3; .24 mm frosted plastic	

001

002

002

003

Stressdesign | 001
DESIGN FIRM | SPECIMEN
Nathan Eaton
DESIGNER(S)
Marc V. Stress
ART DIRECTOR
SSK HR Human Resources Consulting
CLIENT
NOTES
InDesign CS3, Illustrator CS3; Frosted plastic

Evenson Design Group | 002
DESIGN FIRM | SPECIMEN
Mark Sojka
DESIGNER(S)
Stan Evenson
ART DIRECTOR
Mogomedia
CLIENT
NOTES
Illustrator CS3; Synergy Urban Gray, Comp
Green Felt Duplex

WITH creative, llc | 003
DESIGN FIRM | SPECIMEN
Jonathan Gouthier
DESIGNER(S)
WITH creative, llc
CLIENT
NOTES
Illustrator CS3; French Paper Smart White 100 lb. Cover

Biz-R	*001*
DESIGN FIRM	SPECIMEN
Paul Warren	
DESIGNER(S)	
Blair Thomson	
ART DIRECTOR	
Amanda Marsden	
CLIENT	

C3-Creative Consumer Concepts	*002*
DESIGN FIRM	SPECIMEN
Chris Evans, Ed Schlittenhardt	
DESIGNER(S)	
Doug Kubert, Matt Loehrer	
ART DIRECTOR	
C3-Creative Consumer Concepts	
CLIENT	

NOTES

Illustrator CS3; 10.5 x 2 Mohawk DT 100 lb. Cover, Prints 6 over 4, foil stamped (new die), Die cut (used die on hand), finish trim

GLIMMERY EXCELLENTIOUS

- SPOT VARNISHED
- METALLIC INKS
- FOIL-STAMPED

- EASY TO STARE AT
- SOMETIMES REFLECTIVE

KEY CHARACTERISTICS

A highly nocturnal genus of *Cardious de Business* is *Glimmery Excellentious*. These creatures excel in low-light scenarios where they have learned to take the glimmers of light that shine on them, and reflect it with extraordinary success. Some examples use spotted varnish coatings to contrast their normally dull complexions and set them apart without being too loud. Others are more forthright by utilizing foil stamps or metallic inks to create a unique sheen to their coats. Regardless of their approach, *Glimmery Excellentious* goes to great lengths to differentiate themselves from the rest of their kingdom. While not as breathtaking as they appear in their natural habitats, we have managed to capture some fine examples of these creatures for exhibition on the following pages.

NOTES

glow
GLUTEN FREE

Jill Brack

(p/f) 800 497 7434
(m)   917 573 2388

jill@glowglutenfree.com
glowglutenfree.com

No. 17   Watch Your Sales Glow

Do you sell gluten free products? Well get off

your _____ and smell the _____.
          body part   plural noun
This is it baby, the latest, _____ thing
                              adjective
that's going to rock your bottom-_____.
                                    noun
Stock up today.

KELLY KAMINSKI *principal*

1128 north ashland avenue chicago illinois 60622
312+906+8020   773+235+4747   gripdesign.com

JIM RILEY, CDC PRESIDENT & CEO

contact

T. 314 432 1636
D. 314 802 3525
F. 314 802 3565

address

2463 SCHUETZ ROAD
MARYLAND HEIGHTS
MISSOURI 63043

online

JIMRILEY@
RBOINC.COM

RBOPRINTLOGISTIX
the best at complex

METALMEDIA.LLC
621 South Fifth Avenue
85003
1500
1800

jeff@metalmedia.com

M E T A L

E D I A

Jeff Hebets

the best at complex

001

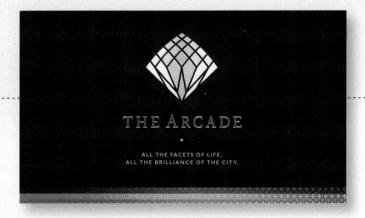

STEVEN J. CLARK SALES ASSOCIATE

816 Olive Street, St. Louis, MO 63101

t. 314 345 1100

sclark@**ARCADELIVING.COM**

002

003

maas DESIGN & COMMUNICATION

Matthew Van Der Maas_ designer/principal

email_ matt@maasdesign.com   phone_ 248 840 7537   web_ maasdesign.com

Di Depux	001
DESIGN FIRM	SPECIMEN
Despina Bournele	
DESIGNER(S)	
Despina Bournele	
ART DIRECTOR	
Lucas Politis	
CLIENT	
NOTES	
Illustrator CS2; 1 Pantone, glitter foil stamp, diecut, perrakis gold 310 gsm	

TOKY Branding + Design	002
DESIGN FIRM	SPECIMEN
Benjamin Franklin, Karin Soukup	
DESIGNER(S)	
Eric Thoelke	
ART DIRECTOR	
The Arcade	
CLIENT	
NOTES	
Creative Suite, Quark; Mohawk Superfine Ultrawhite, embossed, foil stamped	

Maas Design	003
DESIGN FIRM	SPECIMEN
Matthew Van Der Maas	
DESIGNER(S)	
Matthew Van Der Maas	
ART DIRECTOR	
Maas Design	
CLIENT	
NOTES	
InDesign CS3; Yupo coated	

Brainforest, Inc.
DESIGN FIRM

001
SPECIMEN

Drew Larson, Kim Knoll
DESIGNER(S)

Nils Bunde
ART DIRECTOR

RWH Myers
CLIENT

NOTES

Illustrator CS3, InDesign CS3; Strathmore
Writing 100 lb. Cover

Waterform Design Inc.
DESIGN FIRM

002
SPECIMEN

Masayo Nai
DESIGNER(S)

Masayo Nai
ART DIRECTOR

Waterform Design Inc.
CLIENT

NOTES

Illustrator CS3; Logo produced with matte
silver foil stamps

Miller + Miller
DESIGN FIRM

003
SPECIMEN

Ryan Miller, Sarah Miller
DESIGNER(S)

J. D. Thompson
CLIENT

NOTES

Illustrator CS3; Brown Plike 122 lb. coated Paper

Archrival
DESIGN FIRM

004
SPECIMEN

Clint Runge
DESIGNER(S)

Clint Runge
ART DIRECTOR

Nomad Lounge
CLIENT

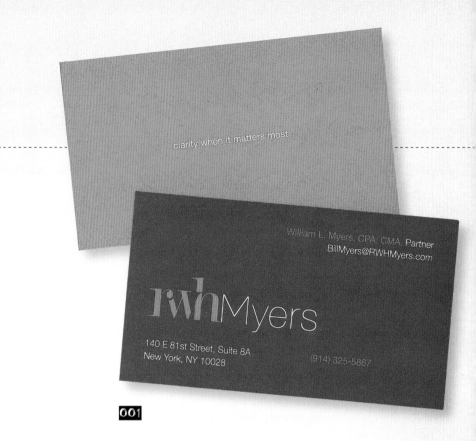

clarity when it matters most

William L. Myers, CPA, CMA, Partner
BillMyers@RWHMyers.com

rwhMyers

140 E 81st Street, Suite 8A
New York, NY 10028

(914) 325-5867

001

Masayo Nai
Waterform Design Inc
P+F 212 684 5012
m_nai@masayonai.com
www.masayonai.com

002

J.D. Thompson
General Contractor

P · 435-673-3117
C · 435-705-0515
F · 435-673-2967

jdt@jdthompsonhomes.com

1722 E. 280 North St.

Studio Q One

St. George, UT 84790

jdthompsonhomes.com

003

NOMAD LOUNGE

MADELINE JAHN
P 462 884 1231 · 1013 JONES OMAHA

MADELINE.JAHN@NOMADLOUNGE.COM

004

glow
GLUTEN FREE

Jill Brack

(p/f) 800 497 7434
(m)   917 573 2388

jill@glowglutenfree.com
glowglutenfree.com

No. 17   Watch Your Sales Glow

Do you sell gluten free products? Well get off

your _____ and smell the _____.
        body part   *plural noun*

This is it baby, the latest, _____ thing
                              adjective

that's going to rock your bottom-_____
                                  noun

Stock up today.

001

✦ heal**ionics**®

INNOVATIVE SOLUTIONS FROM ENGINEERED BIOMATERIALS

Bill Eaton | Chief Financial Officer

T + 1 425.818.1987 x304
C +1 360.921.8611
bill.eaton@healionics.com

14787 NE 95th Street
Redmond, WA 98052

✦ heal**ionics**®

www.healionics.com

002

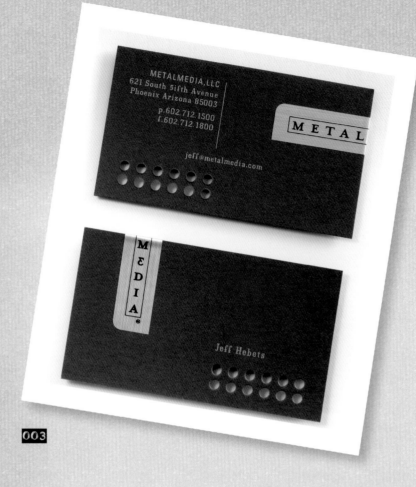

003

Douglas Skipworth
CHIEF EXECUTIVE OFFICER

5100 Wheelis Drive #100
Memphis, Tennessee 38117

dskipworth@redplusinnovations.com
TEL / 901.682.7600   FAX / 901.763.1997

www.redplusinnovations.com

004

Fusing Real Estate Data and Technology

traciedesigns	001
DESIGN FIRM	SPECIMEN
Tracie Valentino	
DESIGNER(S)	
glow gluten free	
CLIENT	
NOTES	
Quark; Esse Pearlized White Smooth 110 lb. coated	

studiovertex	002
DESIGN FIRM	SPECIMEN
Michael Lindsay	
DESIGNER(S)	
Michael Lindsay	
ART DIRECTOR	
Healionics	
CLIENT	
NOTES	
InDesign CS3; Classic Crest Solar White	

Studio Conover	003
DESIGN FIRM	SPECIMEN
Josh Higgins	
DESIGNER(S)	
David Conover	
ART DIRECTOR	
Metal Media	
CLIENT	
NOTES	
InDesign CS3; French construction charcoal die-cut perforation and silk screened metal label	

faculty of design	004
DESIGN FIRM	SPECIMEN
Lucas Charles	
DESIGNER(S)	
Lucas Charles	
ART DIRECTOR	
Douglas Skipworth	
CLIENT	
NOTES	
Illustrator CS3, InDesign CS3	

Miller + Miller
DESIGN FIRM

001
SPECIMEN

Ryan Miller, Sarah Miller
DESIGNER(S)

Osment Enterprises
CLIENT

NOTES

Illustrator CS3; Black Touché .013 in.

TOKY Branding + Design
DESIGN FIRM

002
SPECIMEN

Benjamin Franklin
DESIGNER(S)

Eric Thoelke
ART DIRECTOR

RBO Print Logistix
CLIENT

NOTES

Creative Suite, Quark; Mohawk Superfine Ultrawhite

Fridge Creative
DESIGN FIRM

003
SPECIMEN

Anna Hilton
DESIGNER(S)

Michael Boston
ART DIRECTOR

Hoxton Street Studios
CLIENT

NOTES

Illustrator CS3

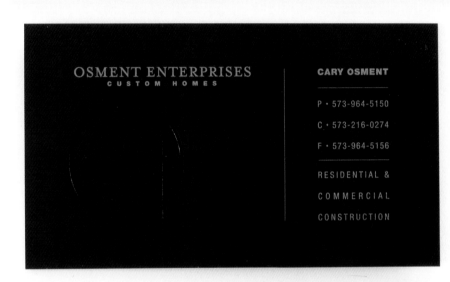

001

JIM RILEY, CDC PRESIDENT & CEO

contact

T. 314 432 1636
D. 314 802 3525
F. 314 802 3565

address

2463 SCHUETZ ROAD
MARYLAND HEIGHTS
MISSOURI 63043

online

JIMRILEY@
RBOINC.COM

RBOPRINTLOGISTIX
the best at complex

the best at complex

002

003

LA FONDA DEL SOL

200 Park Avenue
New York, NY 10166
tel. 212 867 6767
www.patinagroup.com

KELLY KAMINSKI *principal*

1128 north ashland avenue chicago illinois 60622

T 312+906+8020   F 773+235+4747

E kelly@gripdesign.com   W gripdesign.com

002

PURE

NORTH
480.355.0999

NORTH FAX
480.355.0996

SOUTH
480.947.1077

SOUTH FAX
480.947.1087

PURESOUTH@GARDMG.COM
PURENORTH@GARDMG.COM

PURESUSHIBAR.COM

NORTH ▲ 20567 N HAYDEN RD STE 100 SCOTTSDALE AZ 85255
SOUTH ▼ 7343 E SCOTTSDALE MALL STE 1000 SCOTTSDALE AZ 85251

003

Mirko Ilić Corp.	*001*
DESIGN FIRM	SPECIMEN
Mirko Ilić, Jee-eun Lee	
DESIGNER(S)	
Mirko Ilić	
ART DIRECTOR	
Patina Restaurant Group	
CLIENT	
NOTES	
Illustrator CS3	

Grip Design	*002*
DESIGN FIRM	SPECIMEN
Kelly Kaminski, Josh Blaylock	
DESIGNER(S)	
Kelly Kaminski	
ART DIRECTOR	
Grip Design	
CLIENT	
NOTES	
Illustrator CS3	

Tomko Design	*003*
DESIGN FIRM	SPECIMEN
Mike Tomko	
DESIGNER(S)	
Mike Tomko	
ART DIRECTOR	
Pure Sushi Bar and Dining	
CLIENT	
NOTES	
Illustrator CS3; Classic Crest Smooth	

MINIMAL DESIGNIOUS

- BALANCED NEGATIVE SPACE
- SOFT SPOKEN
- CONFIDENT
- QUIETLY AGGRESSIVE
- BEAUTIFULLY SIMPLE

KEY CHARACTERISTICS

While other genera of *Cardious de Business* try to compete for attention, one grouping is unique in its less-is-more attitude. These examples of *Minimal Designious* attempt to maximize their impact by minimizing their outward noise. Sometimes overlooked, these examples carefully compose themselves to be among the strongest specimens in their environment. Using a balance of typography, image, and negative space, *Minimal Designious* often lulls its flashier competition into a false sense of security while quietly stalking the competition. This exhibit was able to capture the finest examples of these confidently understated creatures for display on the following pages.

NOTES

JEFFREY WRIGHT
jeff@actiumpartners.com

III EAST BROADWAY STE 390
SALT LAKE CITY, UTAH 84III

tel **8OI 983 6700**
dir 8OI 994 5650
fax 8OI 983 6705

.mirand
DIRECTOR

broken heart blues

leadstar
LEADERSHIP BY ANGIE & COURTNEY

PO Box 32
Fairfax, VA 220
T (800) 381 77
T (703) 273 7
F (703) 273 7
liz@leadsta
www.leadsta

© 2008 www.tigrafik.be
& "titi"superster"

LARA MIKLA.
FOOD STYLI

JOHN   FERN

graphic designer
847.609.4742

**CMD+
SHIFT**
DESIGN

**CREATIVE
PITCH.** ORG

DON'T THROW AWAY
YOUR CHANCE TO HELP.

CREATIVE
2211 N. Elston Ave. Suite 309, Chicago, IL 60614

t: 773.395.2500 | info @creativepitch.org | creativepitch.org

Creative Pitch is an initiative of BFriend Inc.,
an Illinois NFP Corporation

FSC

Ken P. Flower
senior manager woodward design+build
kflower@woodwarddesignbuild.com
504 628 4697 mobile

504 822 6443 tel
504 822 9493 fax

1019 South Dupre Street
New Orleans LA 70125

woodwarddesignbuild.com

woodward engineering group
structural & civil

001

2020vision
ENERGY + SECURITY SOLUTIONS

John Charles
Development Director

8403 Colesville Road, Suite 860
Silver Spring, Maryland 20910
www.2020vision.org

+ Telephone 301-587-1782
+ Facsimile 301-587-1848
+ john@2020vision.org

002

003

004

45A Arab Street Singapore 199743
(Entrance Via 16A Haji Lane)
Tel. (65) 6294 1505

www.billetdouxstore.com

Zande + Newman Design	001
DESIGN FIRM	SPECIMEN
Loren Stephens, Jan Bertman	
DESIGNER(S)	
Adam Newman	
ART DIRECTOR	
Woodward Design + Build	
CLIENT	
NOTES	
InDesign CS3; Sapi Lustro Dull 120 lb.	

MSDS	002
DESIGN FIRM	SPECIMEN
Jennifer Lapardo	
DESIGNER(S)	
Matthew Schwartz	
ART DIRECTOR	
2020 Vision	
CLIENT	
NOTES	
CS3; Cougar	

Rule29 Creative	003
DESIGN FIRM	SPECIMEN
Kara Ayaram	
DESIGNER(S)	
Justin Ahrens	
ART DIRECTOR	
MacDonald Photography	
CLIENT	
NOTES	
InDesign CS3	

Royal Fly LLP	004
DESIGN FIRM	SPECIMEN
Eunice Wee	
DESIGNER(S)	
Fabian Lim, Ken Tan	
ART DIRECTOR	
Billet Doux	
CLIENT	
NOTES	
Illustrator CS3; 230 lb. Artcard, Matte lamination	

Tomko Design	001
DESIGN FIRM	SPECIMEN
Mike Tomko	
DESIGNER(S)	
Mike Tomko	
ART DIRECTOR	
Candelaria Design	
CLIENT	
NOTES	
Illustrator CS3; Classic Crest Smooth	

Selena Chen + Michael Tam	002
DESIGN FIRM	SPECIMEN
Selena Chen + Michael Tam	
DESIGNER(S)	
Selena Chen + Michael Tam	
ART DIRECTOR	
Projet F	
CLIENT	
NOTES	
Photoshop CS3, InDesign CS3; Scanned real hair for art	

212-BIG-BOLT	003
DESIGN FIRM	SPECIMEN
Pieter Woudt	
DESIGNER(S)	
Pieter Woudt	
ART DIRECTOR	
Kikkerland	
CLIENT	
NOTES	
Illustrator CS3; Uncoated paper	

Grip Design	004
DESIGN FIRM	SPECIMEN
Josh Blaylock	
DESIGNER(S)	
Kelly Kaminski	
ART DIRECTOR	
Cassiday Schade	
CLIENT	
NOTES	
Illustrator CS3	

MSDS	005
DESIGN FIRM	SPECIMEN
Niall O'Kelly	
DESIGNER(S)	
Matthew Schwartz	
ART DIRECTOR	
MSDS	
CLIENT	
NOTES	
CS3; Mohawk Superfine 130 lb.	

P 602 604 2001   P₂ 877 923 4CDA   F 602 604 2002

PATRICK BANKS
PROJECT MANAGER
patrick@candelariadesign.com

4450 NORTH 12TH STREET   SUITE 278   PHOENIX, ARIZONA 85014
www.candelariadesign.com

001

Projet F

002

Ken
Hair Stylist
917.558.1132

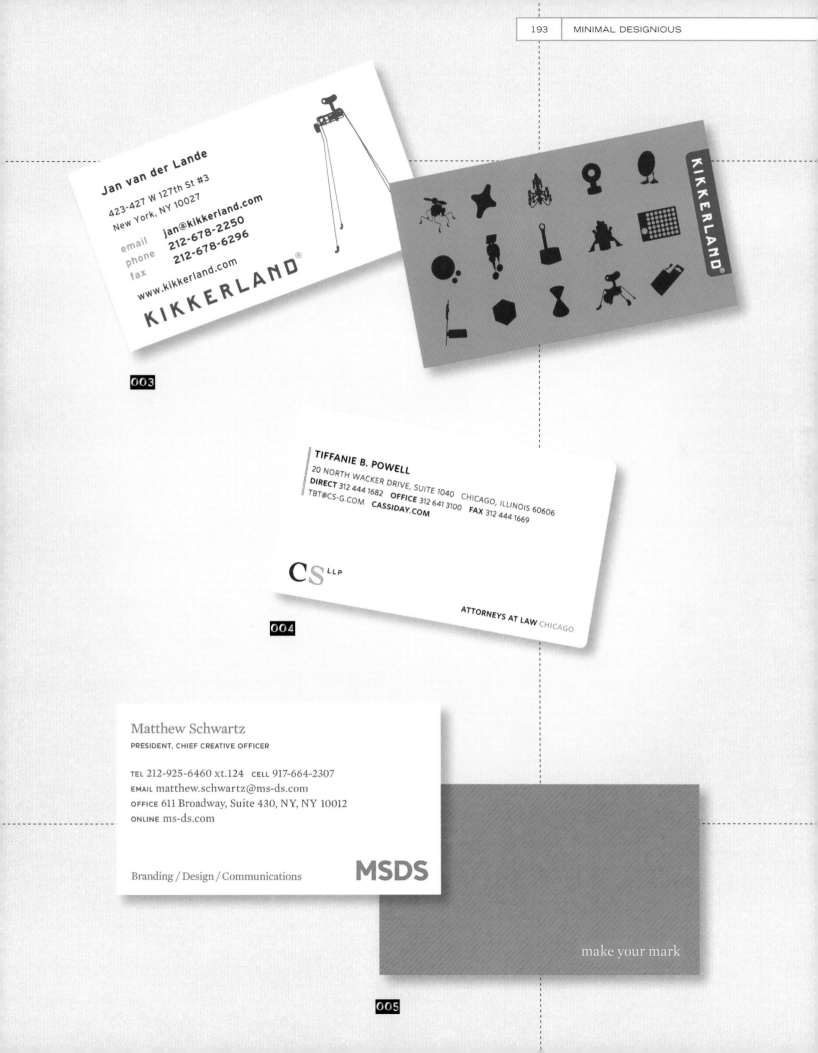

Jan van der Lande

423-427 W 127th St #3
New York, NY 10027

email   **jan@kikkerland.com**
phone   **212-678-2250**
fax   **212-678-6296**

www.kikkerland.com

KIKKERLAND®

KIKKERLAND®

003

TIFFANIE B. POWELL
20 NORTH WACKER DRIVE, SUITE 1040   CHICAGO, ILLINOIS 60606
DIRECT 312 444 1682   **OFFICE** 312 641 3100   **FAX** 312 444 1669
TBT@CS-G.COM   **CASSIDAY.COM**

CS LLP

ATTORNEYS AT LAW CHICAGO

004

Matthew Schwartz

PRESIDENT, CHIEF CREATIVE OFFICER

TEL 212-925-6460 xt.124   CELL 917-664-2307
EMAIL matthew.schwartz@ms-ds.com
OFFICE 611 Broadway, Suite 430, NY, NY 10012
ONLINE ms-ds.com

Branding / Design / Communications   **MSDS**

make your mark

005

Costas Striftos
Managing Director
6973 431690
cstriftos@rockguide.gr

www.rockguide.gr

001

A. BURT HARLAN
Owner
Winegrower Relations

949.275.4977
ArdenBurt@BrianArdenWines.com
www.BrianArdenWines.com

002

003

004

Di Depux	001
DESIGN FIRM	SPECIMEN
Despina Bournele	
DESIGNER(S)	
Despina Bournele	
ART DIRECTOR	
Costas Striftos	
CLIENT	
NOTES	
Illustrator CS2; CMYK, velvet grade 350 gsm, spot UV	

Damion Hickman Design	002
DESIGN FIRM	SPECIMEN
Damion Hickman	
DESIGNER(S)	
Damion Hickman	
ART DIRECTOR	
Brian Arden Wines	
CLIENT	
NOTES	
Illustrator CS3	

CMD+SHIFT Design	003
DESIGN FIRM	SPECIMEN
Liz Andrade	
DESIGNER(S)	
Liz Andrade	
ART DIRECTOR	
CMD+SHIFT Design	
CLIENT	
NOTES	
Illustrator CS3	

Grip Design	004
DESIGN FIRM	SPECIMEN
Josh Blaylock, Ken Otsuka	
DESIGNER(S)	
Kelly Kaminski	
ART DIRECTOR	
Boka Restaurant Group	
CLIENT	
NOTES	
Illustrator CS3	

Handcrafted Media	001
DESIGN FIRM	SPECIMEN
Miles McIlhargie	
DESIGNER(S)	
Miles McIlhargie	
ART DIRECTOR	
Lancelotta Consulting	
CLIENT	
NOTES	
Illustrator CS3, InDesign; 2 PMS, 220 lb. stock	

Grip Design	002
DESIGN FIRM	SPECIMEN
Kelly Kaminski	
DESIGNER(S)	
Kelly Kaminski	
ART DIRECTOR	
The Few Institute	
CLIENT	
NOTES	
Illustrator CS3	

FUNNEL: Eric Kass : Utilitarian + Commercial + Fine : Art	003
DESIGN FIRM	SPECIMEN
Eric Kass	
DESIGNER(S)	
Ray Roman Films	
CLIENT	
NOTES	
Illustrator CS3; Offset litho	

Selena Chen	004
DESIGN FIRM	SPECIMEN
Selena Chen	
DESIGNER(S)	
Selena Chen	
ART DIRECTOR	
Selena Chen	
CLIENT	
NOTES	
Photoshop CS3, InDesign CS3	

Maas Design	005
DESIGN FIRM	SPECIMEN
Matthew Van Der Maas	
DESIGNER(S)	
Matthew Van Der Maas	
ART DIRECTOR	
Kinwood Landscape	
CLIENT	
NOTES	
InDesign CS3; Classic Crest uncoated	

KEVIN LANCELOTTA, PhD
119 Braintree Street №408
Boston MA 02134
617 320-2021
kevin@lancelottaconsulting.com
www.lancelottaconsulting.com

LANCELOTTA
CONSULTING

001

CHARISSE WASHINGTON RN
MEDICAL AESTHETICIAN, MAKEUP ARTIST

phone 312.202.0882 *fax* 312.564.4585
875 NORTH MICHIGAN AVENUE SUITE 3850 CHICAGO IL 60611

WWW.FEWINSTITUTE.COM

002

THE FEW INSTITUTE
for AESTHETIC PLASTIC SURGERY

RAY ROMAN
FILMS
award winning cinematography

RAY@RAYROMANFILMS.COM

5340 NORTH FEDERAL HIGHWAY SUITE 104
LIGHTHOUSE POINT FLORIDA 33064
TF 800 948 3914 PH 786 236 0743

RAYROMANFILMS.COM

003

004

Selena Chen
graphic designer

c 646.421.8284
h 212.966.0898
scrabbit@gmail.com

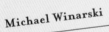

Michael Winarski   *project manager*

Kinwood Landscape
7104 Crossroads Blvd. Ste 104
Brentwood, TN 37027

Office: 615·373·3809
Fax: 615·373·3810
Cell: 586·557·8019
michael@kinwoodlandscape.com

005

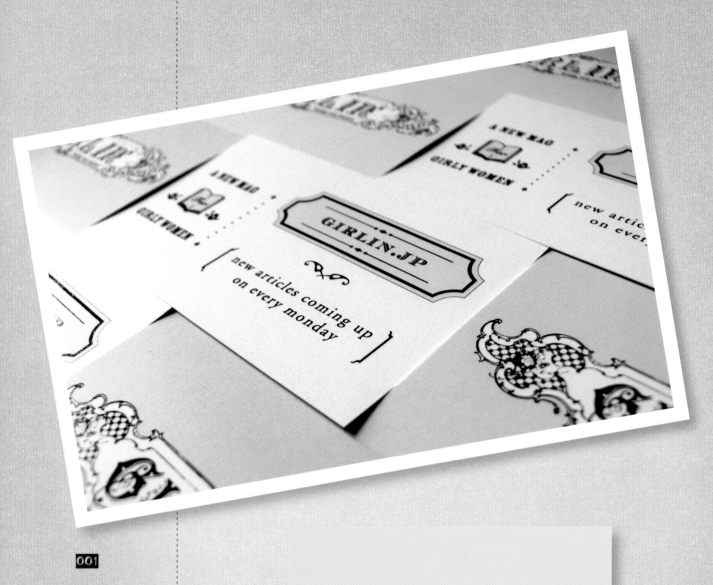

001

graphic designer
847.609.4742

johnferndesign.com
jfern@johnferndesign.com

002

003

designer

Sophy Sorim Lee
tel: (917) 613-3598
e-mail: slee10@sva.edu

HI(NY), LLC	001
DESIGN FIRM	SPECIMEN
Hitomi Watanabe, Iku Oyamada	
DESIGNER(S)	
Hitomi Watanabe, Iku Oyamada	
ART DIRECTOR	
GIRLIN'	
CLIENT	
NOTES	
Illustrator CS3; Matte paper	

John Fern	002
DESIGN FIRM	SPECIMEN
John Fern	
DESIGNER(S)	
John Fern	
CLIENT	
NOTES	
Illustrator CS3	

Sophy (Sorim) Lee	003
DESIGN FIRM	SPECIMEN
Sophy (Sorim) Lee	
DESIGNER(S)	
NOTES	
Illustrator CS3, Photoshop CS3	

FUNNEL: Eric Kass : Utilitarian +
Commercial + Fine : Art | 001
DESIGN FIRM | SPECIMEN

Eric Kass
DESIGNER(S)

Saarinen Artist Reps
CLIENT

NOTES
Illustrator CS3; Letterpress

TOKY Branding + Design | 002
DESIGN FIRM | SPECIMEN

Jamie Banks-George
DESIGNER(S)

Eric Thoelke
ART DIRECTOR

Lead Star
CLIENT

NOTES
Illustrator CS3; Mohawk Superfine Ultrawhite Smooth

TOKY Branding + Design | 003
DESIGN FIRM | SPECIMEN

Benjamin Franklin
DESIGNER(S)

Eric Thoelke
ART DIRECTOR

Ferguson & Katzman Photography
CLIENT

NOTES
Creative Suite; Mohawk Superfine Ultrawhite

TOKY Branding + Design | 004
DESIGN FIRM | SPECIMEN

Travis Brown, Jamie Banks-George
DESIGNER(S)

Eric Thoelke
ART DIRECTOR

CWE Hospitality Services, LLC
CLIENT

NOTES
Illustrator CS3; Mohawk Superfine White Eggshell

ERIKA SHELDON

1680 VINE STREET SUITE 1208
HOLLYWOOD CALIFORNIA 90028

ERIKA@SAARINEN.TV

323 460 2320

001

Liz Lamirand
EXECUTIVE DIRECTOR

leadstar™
LEADERSHIP BY ANGIE & COURTNEY

PO Box 328
Fairfax, VA 22038
T (800) 381 7780
T (703) 273 7280
F (703) 273 7281
liz@leadstar.us
www.leadstar.us

002

Leadership is not about
power, prestige or perks.
It's about responsibility.

A leader is someone
who influences outcomes
and inspires others.

www.leadstar.us

SCOTT FERGUSON

FERGUSON@FKPHOTO.COM
PHONE 314.241.3811

Ferguson & Katzman Photography

FK

FKPHOTO.COM

2745 LOCUST STREET, 2ND FLOOR, ST. LOUIS, MISSOURI 63103

003

DAVID SUTTON
Senior Vice President & Chief Financial Officer

CWE HOSPITALITY SERVICES, LLC.

212 N. KINGSHIGHWAY BLVD.
SAINT LOUIS, MISSOURI 63108
tel 314 633 1017 *fax* 314 633 3077

dsutton@chaseparkplaza.com

CWE HOSPITALITY
SERVICES, LLC.

004

Lucas Charles
lcharles@facultyofdesign.com

Faculty of Design

2143 Abergeldie Drive
Memphis, Tennessee 38119
facultyofdesign.com
901.679.5276

001

SOHO
SALON

002

valerie
gonzales
hair stylist
602.820.5191

SOHO
SALON

Reach. Empower. Dream
a world without HIV

Teresa Franklin   **AIDS Resource Center Ohio**
Chair   15 West Fourth Street, Suite 200
              Dayton, Ohio 45402
              C 937 902 0289
              dfrank1430@aol.com

design & dine 2008

003

HILL INVESTMENT GROUP

Matt Hall
Principal

matt@hillinvestmentgroup.com

7701 Forsyth Blvd
Suite 350
St. Louis, MO 63105
tel. 314 448 4023
fax. 314 448 4027

HILL INVESTMENT GROUP
Take the long view

004

WILLIAM K. HELLMUTH AIA, LEED® AP
President

bill.hellmuth@hok.com
t +1 202 944 1519 f +1 202 339 8800 m +1 202 288 6143
HOK Canal House, 3223 Grace Street, N.W. | Washington, DC 20007 USA

005

Faculty of Design	*001*
DESIGN FIRM	SPECIMEN
Lucas Charles	
DESIGNER(S)	
Lucas Charles	
ART DIRECTOR	
Faculty of Design	
CLIENT	
NOTES	
Illustrator CS3	

tasteofinkstudios.com	*002*
DESIGN FIRM	SPECIMEN
Nathan Mummert	
DESIGNER(S)	
Nathan Mummert	
ART DIRECTOR	
Soho Salon	
CLIENT	
NOTES	
Photoshop CS3; 15 pt. silk lamination, spot varnish	

Real Art Design Group	*003*
DESIGN FIRM	SPECIMEN
Saundra Marcel, Crystal Dennis	
DESIGNER(S)	
AIDS Resource Center Ohio	
CLIENT	
NOTES	
Illustrator CS3; Cougar Opaque	

TOKY Branding + Design	*004*
DESIGN FIRM	SPECIMEN
Benjamin Franklin	
DESIGNER(S)	
Eric Thoelke	
ART DIRECTOR	
Hill Investment Group	
CLIENT	
NOTES	
Creative Suite, Quark; Mohawk Superfine White Eggshell	

TOKY Branding + Design	*005*
DESIGN FIRM	SPECIMEN
Katy Fischer, Eric Thoelke	
DESIGNER(S)	
Eric Thoelke	
ART DIRECTOR	
HOK	
CLIENT	
NOTES	
Creative Suite; Mohawk Options 100 lb., white	

| Square Feet Design | 001 |
| DESIGN FIRM | SPECIMEN |

Lauren Marwil
DESIGNER(S)

Lauren Marwil
ART DIRECTOR

Square Feet Design
CLIENT

NOTES

Illustrator CS3; Mohawk Superfine
Ultrawhite 130 lb. Cover

| Square Feet Design | 002 |
| DESIGN FIRM | SPECIMEN |

Michelle Snyder
DESIGNER(S)

Lauren Marwil
ART DIRECTOR

Domain Companies / The Preserve
CLIENT

NOTES

Illustrator CS3; Mohawk Superfine
Ultrawhite 130 lb. Cover

| Prime Studio | 003 |
| DESIGN FIRM | SPECIMEN |

Jason Mannix, Lindsay Krembs
DESIGNER(S)

Stuart Harvey Lee
ART DIRECTOR

Prime Studio
CLIENT

NOTES

Illustrator CS3

| Afterhours Group | 004 |
| DESIGN FIRM | SPECIMEN |

Fedra Carina Meredith
DESIGNER(S)

Fedra Carina Meredith
ART DIRECTOR

Afterhours Group
CLIENT

NOTES

Illustrator CS3, InDesign CS3; Neenah Classic Crest 2/2
spot metallic white opaque ink, embossed

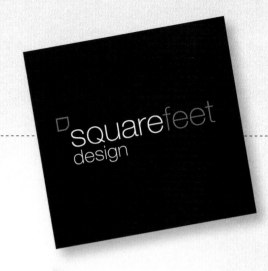

laurenmarwil

11 Park Place
Suite 1705
New York, NY 10007
646.237.2828 x120
646.349.5391 fax
lmarwil@squarefeetdesign.com
squarefeetdesign.com

001

002

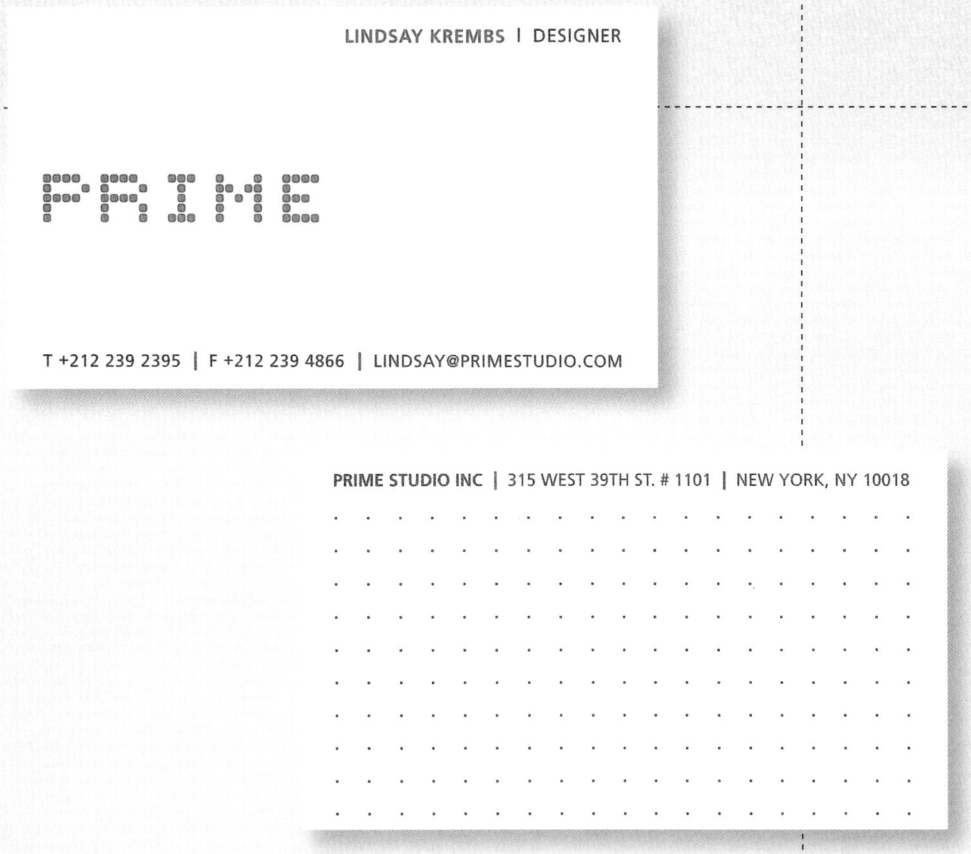

LINDSAY KREMBS | DESIGNER

PRIME

T +212 239 2395 | F +212 239 4866 | LINDSAY@PRIMESTUDIO.COM

PRIME STUDIO INC | 315 WEST 39TH ST. # 1101 | NEW YORK, NY 10018

003

004

eric meredith
managing director

8185 e. lowry boulevard   303.340.0048 ph
ste. 103 • denver 80230   720.212.5056 cel   eric@afterhoursgroup.com
afterhoursgroup.com

afterhours group
DENVER

Anna Shea
CHOCOLATES

TELE   FACS
602 604 3132   602 604 2002
WWW.ILCORTILE-AZ.COM

MARK CANDELARIA
PARTNER
CELL 602 791 9336

MAILING
POST OFFICE BOX 7400
PHOENIX, ARIZONA 85011

LOCATION
4114 NORTH TWENTY-EIGHTH STREET
PHOENIX, ARIZONA 85016

ILCORTILE
THE COURTYARD
EST. 2006

002

Debra Jenrette

877.70.ANNASHEA

THE ARBORETUM OF
SOUTH BARRINGTON
100 W. HIGGINS RD., STE E5
SOUTH BARRINGTON, IL 60010

ANNASHEACHOCOLATES.COM
DEBRA@ANNASHEACHOCOLATES.COM

001

BOOST rewards

Michael Emoff
CEO
michael.emoff@boostrewards.com

811 East Fourth Street
Dayton, Ohio 45402
p: 800 324 9756 f: 877 408 7786

www.boostrewards.com

003

katrin.schnabl@4lines.org

4LINES

004

Ten26 Design Group		001
DESIGN FIRM		SPECIMEN
Kelly Demakis		
DESIGNER(S)		
Kelly Demakis		
ART DIRECTOR		
Anna Shea Chocolates		
CLIENT		
NOTES		
Illustrator CS3; Fibermark Touché		

Tomko Design		002
DESIGN FIRM		SPECIMEN
Mike Tomko		
DESIGNER(S)		
Mike Tomko		
ART DIRECTOR		
Il Cortile		
CLIENT		
NOTES		
Illustrator CS3; Classic Crest		

Real Art Design Group		003
DESIGN FIRM		SPECIMEN
Jennifer Gobrail		
DESIGNER(S)		
Shumsky Boost Rewards		
CLIENT		
NOTES		
Illustrator CS3; Starwhite Vicksburg, Tiara Smooth		

Faust		004
DESIGN FIRM		SPECIMEN
Bob Faust		
DESIGNER(S)		
Bob Faust		
ART DIRECTOR		
4 Lines		
CLIENT		
NOTES		
InDesign CS3; Mohawk Superfine Cover		

Brainforest, Inc.	001
DESIGN FIRM	SPECIMEN
Drew Larson	
DESIGNER(S)	
Nils Bunde	
ART DIRECTOR	
Creative Pitch	
CLIENT	
NOTES	
Illustrator CS3, InDesign CS3; Sappi McCoy 80 lb. Cover	

The Creative Method	002
DESIGN FIRM	SPECIMEN
Andi Yanto	
DESIGNER(S)	
Tony Ibbotson	
ART DIRECTOR	
Restaurant Botanica	
CLIENT	
NOTES	
Illustrator CS3; 350 gsm silk artboard from K. W. Doggett	

Adapter Design	003
DESIGN FIRM	SPECIMEN
Justin Paluch	
DESIGNER(S)	
Justin Paluch	
ART DIRECTOR	
Adapter Design	
CLIENT	
NOTES	
Illustrator CS3; International Paper 12 pt. gloss card stock spot matte coating	

Oxide Design Co.	004
DESIGN FIRM	SPECIMEN
Joe Sparano, Drew Davies	
DESIGNER(S)	
Drew Davies	
ART DIRECTOR	
Film Streams	
CLIENT	
NOTES	
InDesign CS3, Photoshop CS3; Gilbert Oxford	

akrok design	005
DESIGN FIRM	SPECIMEN
hans akrok	
DESIGNER(S)	
hans akrok	
ART DIRECTOR	
akrok design	
CLIENT	
NOTES	
Illustrator CS3; HP adv. glossy photo paper, Navy blue Canford card, Letratec (adhesive), steel ruler, craft knife	

001

002

INTELLIGENT DESIGN

JUSTIN PALUCH
Principal

justin@adapterdesign.com
720.988.8782

003

PO BOX 8485
OMAHA, NE 68108-0485
(402) 933-0259
FILMSTREAMS.ORG

FILM STR

ART FORM · DEVOTED TO THE PRESENTATION AND DISCUSS

STREAMS

OMAHA'S OWN
NONPROFIT CINEMA
(402) 933-0259
INFO@FILMSTREAMS.ORG

ND DISCUSSION OF FILM AS AN ART FORM · DEVOTED TO TH

004

005

BRIAN BALMERT / OWNER

301 OCCIDENTAL AVENUE SOUTH
SEATTLE, WASHINGTON 98104
T 206 859 6492
F 206 859 6493
E BRIAN@ORNAMO.COM
WWW.ORNAMO.COM

ORNAMO

001

Rachel Cunha

Senior Designer

TIHANY DESIGN

135 West 27th Street

New York, NY 10001

tel: 212 366 5544

fax: 212 366 4302

rcunha@tihanydesign.com

002

FFKR
ARCHITECTS

JILL CALDER

boque building
730 pacific avenue
salt lake city, utah 84104

o 801-521-6186 **d** 80
f 801-539-1916 **c** 8

jcalder@ffkr.com

FFKR
ARCHITECTS

JILL CALDER

boque building
730 pacific avenue
salt lake city, utah 84104

o 801-521-6186 **d** 801-517-4321
f 801-539-1916 **c** 801-910-9185

jcalder@ffkr.com

003

004

005

Netra Nei	001
DESIGN FIRM	SPECIMEN
Netra Nei	
DESIGNER(S)	
Ornamo	
CLIENT	
NOTES	
Illustrator CS3; Starwhite Tiara Vellum 130 lb. Cover	

Mirko Ilić Corp.	002
DESIGN FIRM	SPECIMEN
Mirko Ilić	
DESIGNER(S)	
Mirko Ilić	
ART DIRECTOR	
Tihany Design	
CLIENT	
NOTES	
Illustrator CS3	

Struck	003
DESIGN FIRM	SPECIMEN
Shayna Proctor	
DESIGNER(S)	
Ryan Goodwin, Peder Singleton	
ART DIRECTOR	
FFKR	
CLIENT	
NOTES	
Illustrator CS3, InDesign CS3; Mohawk Navajo	

The Creative Method	004
DESIGN FIRM	SPECIMEN
Andi Yanto	
DESIGNER(S)	
Tony Ibbotson	
ART DIRECTOR	
Over the Moon Dairy Co.	
CLIENT	
NOTES	
Illustrator CS3, Photoshop CS3; 271 Cambric Linen from K. W. Doggett	

The Creative Method	005
DESIGN FIRM	SPECIMEN
Andi Yanto	
DESIGNER(S)	
Tony Ibbotson	
ART DIRECTOR	
The Wine House & Kitchen	
CLIENT	
NOTES	
Illustrator CS3; Nordset 300 gsm from Raleigh	

Fusedmedia	001
DESIGN FIRM	SPECIMEN
Jared Fusedale	
DESIGNER(S)	
Jared Fusedale	
ART DIRECTOR	
alt tax	
CLIENT	
NOTES	
Illustrator CS3, InDesign CS3	

Wendy Polish	002
DESIGN FIRM	SPECIMEN
Wendy Polish	
DESIGNER(S)	
Wendy Polish	
ART DIRECTOR	
Wonderfolk	
CLIENT	
NOTES	
Illustrator CS3; Tree Free paper, cotton stock, hand letterpress, Pantone: flame red	

Rutka Weadock Design	003
DESIGN FIRM	SPECIMEN
Zach Richter	
DESIGNER(S)	
Anthony Rutka	
ART DIRECTOR	
Bruce Weller Photography	
CLIENT	
NOTES	
InDesign CS3; Cougar 100 lb.	

Studio Tigrafik	004
DESIGN FIRM	SPECIMEN
Laetitia Verhetsel	
DESIGNER(S)	
Laetitia Verhetsel	
ART DIRECTOR	
Studio Tigrafik	
CLIENT	
NOTES	
InDesign CS3; Steinbach 500 gsm, 2-color silk screen, stamp	

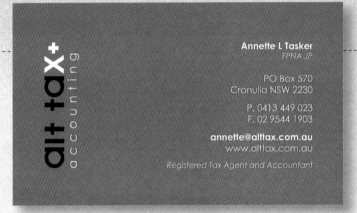

001

wendy polish
323.788.8707
wonderfolk.com

002

WELLER STUDIOS
6508 CRESTWOOD ROAD
BALTIMORE MD 21239

BRUCE WELLER   410.235.4200

PHOTOGRAPHER   WELLERSTUDIOS@COMCAST.NET

WWW.BRUCEWELLER.COM

STUNT DOUBLE

003

LAETITIA VERHETSEL
EDWARD PYNAERTKAAI 115 B
9000 GENT
0479 35 33 82

004

© 2008 www.tigrafik.be
& "liti"superster"

001

ACTIUM
PARTNERS
L + L + C

JEFFREY WRIGHT
jeff@actiumpartners.com

III EAST BROADWAY STE 390
SALT LAKE CITY, UTAH 84111

tel **801 983 6700**
dir 801 994 5650
fax 801 983 6705

002

DEBRA BOWLES
MANAGING PARTNER

bowles@ECSTASIS.COM
SKYPE: **debra.bowles**

ECSTASIS.COM

CELL **+1.415.518.4501**
LAND **+1.949.709.4102**

ECSTASIS
CONSULTING
LLC

THE AMERICAS   ASIA PACIFIC
EUROPE

JUSTINE WALPOLE
PHOTOGRAPHY

JUSTINE WALPOLE 8 UPPER LANCASTER ROAD
MOBILE 0412 192 238 ASCOT Q 4007 AUSTRALIA
       JW@JUSTINEWALPOLE.COM
       WWW.JUSTINEWALPOLE.COM

003

NATURAMA
moderne naturhistorie

Naturama   Gitte Høegh van Deurs
Dronningemaen 30 Marketingkoordinator
DK-5700 Svendborg

T. 45 . 62 21 06 50 M. 45 . 24 88 62 87
F. 45 . 62 21 84 17 gvd@naturama.dk

www.naturama.dk

004

Struck DESIGN FIRM	*001* SPECIMEN
Kenji Bankhead, Dan Christofferson DESIGNER(S)	
Ryan Goodwin, Peder Singleton ART DIRECTOR	
Actium Partners CLIENT	
NOTES	
Illustrator CS3; Mohawk Superfine	

Chen Design Associates DESIGN FIRM	*002* SPECIMEN
Max Spector DESIGNER(S)	
Joshua Chen / Laurie Carrigan ART DIRECTOR	
Ecstasis Consulting CLIENT	
NOTES	
InDesign CS3; Neenah Environment Ultra Bright White 120 lb. Cover	

Plazma Design DESIGN FIRM	*003* SPECIMEN
Todd Hansson DESIGNER(S)	
Todd Hansson ART DIRECTOR	
Justine Walpole Photography CLIENT	
NOTES	
Illustrator CS3; Hanno Art Silk 350 gsm A2; CMYK, Celloglazed	

Designit DESIGN FIRM	*004* SPECIMEN
Designit DESIGNER(S)	
Designit ART DIRECTOR	
Naturama CLIENT	
NOTES	
Illustrator	

Peter Devenport
Director of Architecture

43 Alfred Street
Mermaid Beach Q 4218
Telephone 07 5526 1100
Facsimile 07 5526 1099
Mobile 0400 000 000
pd@burnsdesign.com.au
www.burnsdesign.com.au

URBAN DESIGN
ARCHITECTURE
INTERIORS
MASTERPLANNING

001

002

Sexty Design
DESIGN FIRM

001
SPECIMEN

Todd Hansson
DESIGNER(S)

Peter Sexty
ART DIRECTOR

Burns Architecture
CLIENT

NOTES

Illustrator CS3; Impress Silk 350 gsm, 2 PMS,
Celloglazed, UV varnish

Neoscape
DESIGN FIRM

002
SPECIMEN

Derek Luciani, Dan Kaplan, Yoonkyung Myung
DESIGNER(S)

Leila Mitchell, Travis Blake
ART DIRECTOR

Neoscape
CLIENT

NOTES

CS; Mohawk Options 130 lb., letterpress

Evenson Design Group
DESIGN FIRM

003
SPECIMEN

Dallas Duncan
DESIGNER(S)

Stan Evenson, Mark Sojka
ART DIRECTOR

David Ari Leon / Sound Mind Music
CLIENT

NOTES

Illustrator CS3; Classic Crest Avalanche White

Plazma Design
DESIGN FIRM

004
SPECIMEN

Todd Hansson
DESIGNER(S)

Todd Hansson
ART DIRECTOR

Studio De Shan
CLIENT

NOTES

Illustrator CS3; Monza Satin 300 gsm, UV varnish,
matte celloglaze

SOUNDMINDMUSIC
Music for all Media

David Ari Leon

310 770 3311
dleon@soundmindmusic.net
www.soundmindmusic.net

003

STUDIO
DE SHAN

DE SHAN VISUAL ARTIST
PO BOX 793 NEW FARM Q 4005
MOBILE (+61) 424 032 164
EMAIL INFO@STUDIODESHAN.COM
WEBSITE STUDIODESHAN.COM

004

DARIAN WELTMAN SWIG
Principal

Article 3
A D V I S O R S

+1.415.885.2750 OFFICE
+1.415.885.2410 FAX
MAIL 400 Spear Street · Suite 106   darian@swigsf.com EMAIL
San Francisco, CA 94105   www.article3.com WEB

SUPPORTING
PHILANTHROPY
PROMOTING
HUMAN RIGHTS

ARTICLE 3
Everyone has the right to life, liberty and security
of person.   THE UNIVERSAL DECLARATION OF HUMAN RIGHTS

001

LIVING ROOM
– PHARMACY –

Greg Oksanen Pharmacist/Owner
204-1530 Cliffe Avenue Courtenay BC V9N 2K4
Tel 250.338.5665 Toll free 1.877.214.6337
Fax 250.338.5855 greg@livingrx.ca www.livingrx.ca

002

003

004

Shelby Designs & Illustrates | 001
DESIGN FIRM | SPECIMEN

Will Yang
DESIGNER(S)

Shelby Putnam Tupper
ART DIRECTOR

Article 3 Advisors
CLIENT

NOTES

InDesign Cs3; Crane Cotton, letterpress

Spring | 002
DESIGN FIRM | SPECIMEN

Perry Chua
DESIGNER(S)

Perry Chua
ART DIRECTOR

Living Room Pharmacy
CLIENT

Westwerk Design | 003
DESIGN FIRM | SPECIMEN

Dan West
DESIGNER(S)

Dan West
ART DIRECTOR

Lara Miklasevics
CLIENT

NOTES

Illustrator CS3

G-Man | 004
DESIGN FIRM | SPECIMEN

Graham Jones
DESIGNER(S)

Graham Jones
ART DIRECTOR

Karen Gaskill
CLIENT

NOTES

Illustrator CS3; Pink metallic foil, Black gloss foil,
uncoated charcoal stock

Robin Easter Design	001
DESIGN FIRM	SPECIMEN

Heather Kerchner
DESIGNER(S)

Robin Easter Reeves
ART DIRECTOR

Three Rivers Market
CLIENT

NOTES
Illustrator CS3; French Speckletone Cream

Robin Easter Design	002
DESIGN FIRM	SPECIMEN

Travis Gray
DESIGNER(S)

Robin Easter Reeves
ART DIRECTOR

East Tennessee Film Commission
CLIENT

NOTES
Freehand

Grip Design	003
DESIGN FIRM	SPECIMEN

Kelly Kaminski
DESIGNER(S)

Kelly Kaminski
ART DIRECTOR

Center for Aesthetics and Plastic Surgery
CLIENT

NOTES
Illustrator CS3; Mohawk Navajo

Travis Blake	004
DESIGN FIRM	SPECIMEN

Travis Blake
DESIGNER(S)

Travis Blake
ART DIRECTOR

White Lighthouse Classic Photography
CLIENT

NOTES
Creative Suite; Mohawk Superfine, blind embossing,
adhesive label

001

002

CENTER FOR
AESTHETICS
— AND —
PLASTIC SURGERY

Bradley P. Bengtson MD

TELEPHONE 616.588.2277
FACSIMILE 616.328.8439

2680 Leonard Street NE
Grand Rapids, Michigan 49525

EMAIL drb@capsmi.com
WEB www.capsmi.com

003

WHITE LIGHTHOUSE
CLASSIC PHOTOGRAPHY

TRAVIS BLAKE
PHOTOGRAPHER — ART DIRECTOR
617.935.1705 INFO@WHITELIGHTHOUSEPHOTO.COM

004

001

002

I won my 5th grade spelling bee. Needless to say, I was on top of the world and looking to solidify my spot as king of the schoolyard. But somehow, somewhere, things went wrong. Very wrong. To this day, I can still hear the kids chanting "Punctuation Paul! Punctuation Paul!" over and over and over again. And the laughing. Oh how they laughed. Admittedly, the headgear and viola didn't help. But little did they know that prestige and glamour would come my way as a writer specializing in marketing and corporate communications. Rubbing shoulders with lawyers, accountants and HR professionals. You know, living the good life. Who's laughing now, Olivia Gillespie of homeroom 5C? **Paul Russell, BA LLB Bretenic Limited, 810 Logan Avenue, Toronto, Ontario, Canada, M4K 3E1 Phone 416 466 8781 Fax 416 466 7190 paul@bretenic.ca**

003

004

Paper Tower		*001*
DESIGN FIRM		SPECIMEN
Brenden Jones, Jon McGrath		
DESIGNER(S)		
Brock Henderson		
ART DIRECTOR		
Paper Tower		
CLIENT		
NOTES		
InDesign CS3; White Cougar 130 lb.		

The Designworks Group		*002*
DESIGN FIRM		SPECIMEN
Tim Green		
DESIGNER(S)		
Whipps Childers Communications, LLC		
CLIENT		

Zync Communications		*003*
DESIGN FIRM		SPECIMEN
Mike Kasperski		
DESIGNER(S)		
Marko Zonta, Mike Kasperski		
ART DIRECTOR		
Bretenic Limited		
CLIENT		
NOTES		
Illustrator CS3; Strathmore Writing		

Bryska212 Design		*004*
DESIGN FIRM		SPECIMEN
Bryan McCloskey		
DESIGNER(S)		
Bryan McCloskey		
ART DIRECTOR		
Willix Developments		
CLIENT		
NOTES		
Illustrator CS3; MXM 15 pt. synthetic paperwhite		

Greco Design
DESIGN FIRM
001
SPECIMEN

André Felipe (Tidé), Bruno Nunes
DESIGNER(S)

Gustavo Greco
ART DIRECTOR

Tutto Sano
CLIENT

NOTES

Illustrator CS3; Couché Matte 300gsm laminate matte,
spot UV varnish

Willoughby Design
DESIGN FIRM
002
SPECIMEN

Nate Hardin
DESIGNER(S)

Ann Willoughby
ART DIRECTOR

Willoughby Design
CLIENT

NOTES

Creative Suite; Letterpress

Rutka Weadock Design
DESIGN FIRM
003
SPECIMEN

Zach Richter
DESIGNER(S)

Anthony Rutka
ART DIRECTOR

Peabody Press
CLIENT

NOTES

Illustrator CS3; Crane's Lettra/Gmund

Murillo Design, Inc.
DESIGN FIRM
004
SPECIMEN

Rolando G. Murillo
DESIGNER(S)

Rolando G. Murillo
ART DIRECTOR

Garza Architects
CLIENT

001

002

003

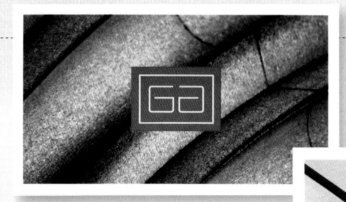

004

JESSE GARZA, AIA > Principal
jgarza@garzaarchitects.com

GARZA ARCHITECTS

V 210.271.3222 F 210.271.3233
816 Camaron, Suite 2.15
San Antonio, TX 78212

MARK JOSEPH
C A K E S

25 JAY STREET #404   T 718.643.8216
BROOKLYN NY 11201   F 718.643.8232
D.U.M.B.O.

WWW.MARKJOSEPHCAKES.COM
INFO@MARKJOSEPHCAKES.COM   BY APPOINTMENT ONLY

001

JANTONE®
3174606063 C

JANTONE®
3174606063 C

JAN
3174

JANTONE®
3174606063 C

JANMICHAEL-B.COM W
INFO@JANMICHAEL-B.COM E

JAN MICHAEL BENNETT / DESIGNER

DATE: ___ / __ / __
___ : _____   A.M. / P.M

☐ EAT / ☐ PLAN / ☐ VIEW CREATIVE
☐ DISCUSS / ☐ CELEBRATE / ☐ OTHER

JANTONE®
3174606063 C

JANTONE®
3174606063 C

002

Ph.D   A Design Office
Michael Hodgson

1524a Cloverfield Blvd.
Santa Monica, CA 90404

310 829 0900
mick@phdla.com

003

manual therapy
OF NASHVILLE

REBECCA LOWE, PT
m-t-n@comcast.net

OFFICE
615 356 1524

CELL
240 751 7578

74 BROOKWOOD TERRACE
NASHVILLE, TN 37205

004

CERTIFIED

AND

FELLOWSHIP

TRAINED

IN

ORTHOPAEDIC

MANUAL

THERAPY

And Creative Production	001
DESIGN FIRM	SPECIMEN
Jennifer Freeouf	
DESIGNER(S)	
J. Freeouf, Vail Palmer	
ART DIRECTOR	
Mark Joseph Cakes	
CLIENT	
NOTES	
InDesign CS3, Illustrator CS3, Photoshop CS3; Strathmore Bright White Writing 80 lb. Cover, duplexed, offset, engraved	

janmichael-b	002
DESIGN FIRM	SPECIMEN
Jan Michael Bennett	
DESIGNER(S)	
Jan Michael Bennett	
ART DIRECTOR	
janmichael-b	
CLIENT	
NOTES	
Illustrator CS3; Neenah Environmental	

Ph.D, A Design Office	003
DESIGN FIRM	SPECIMEN
Michael Hodgson, Derek Schultz	
DESIGNER(S)	
Michael Hodgson	
ART DIRECTOR	
Ph.D, A Design Office	
CLIENT	
NOTES	
InDesign CS3, Photoshop CS3; Crane's Lettra	

Juicebox Designs	004
DESIGN FIRM	SPECIMEN
Jay Smith	
DESIGNER(S)	
Jay Smith	
ART DIRECTOR	
Manual Therapy of Nashville	
CLIENT	
NOTES	
Illustrator CS3, InDesign CS3; Via Vellum Flax 100 lb. coated	

Mirko Ilić Corp.
DESIGN FIRM

001
SPECIMEN

Mirko Ilić
DESIGNER(S)

Mirko Ilić
ART DIRECTOR

Andrew Young & Co.
CLIENT

NOTES

Illustrator CS3

FUNNEL: Eric Kass : Utilitarian +
Commercial + Fine : Art
DESIGN FIRM

002
SPECIMEN

Eric Kass
DESIGNER(S)

Systematiq Research
CLIENT

NOTES

Illustrator CS3; Offset litho, engraved

AFFINA
DESIGN FIRM

003
SPECIMEN

Jessica Zubrzycki
DESIGNER(S)

Renita Van Dusen
ART DIRECTOR

Ellie Kingsbury
CLIENT

NOTES

Illustrator CS3

MINE
DESIGN FIRM

004
SPECIMEN

Christopher Simmons, Tim Belonax
DESIGNER(S)

Christopher Simmons
ART DIRECTOR

Fino
CLIENT

NOTES

Illustrator Cs3; Crane's Lettra 120 lb. coated

Alphabet Arm Design
DESIGN FIRM

005
SPECIMEN

Ryan Frease
DESIGNER(S)

Aaron Belyea
ART DIRECTOR

John Butman
CLIENT

NOTES

Creative Suite; Via Felt

Andrew J. Young

ANDREW YOUNG & CO., INC.
231 Wixon Pond Road
Mahopac, New York 10541

tel. 845.621.2003
fax. 845.622.3550
mobile 917.685.3869

www.andrewyoungandco.com
andrew@andrewyoungandco.co...

ANDREW YOUNG & CO., INC.
global hospitality consultants

001

SYSTEMAT IQ™

R E S E A R C H

CARSON BONECK, CFA \ MANAGING DIRECTOR
cboneck@systematiq-research.com

130 EAST RANDOLPH STREET SUITE 1010 CHICAGO IL 60601

P 312.233.7152 \ C 312.909.1468

SYS·TEM·AT·IQ [sìstə máttik]

A Standard and Poor's Capital IQ Business

002

003

DRAGO HERMAN
MANAGING PARTNER

+1 415 699 7049
HERMAN @ FINEFINO.COM

2719 PACIFIC AVENUE
SAN FRANCISCO, CA 94115
UNITED STATES

004

IDEA PLATFORMS

The **Butman Company** Inc.

Janine Evans PROJECT MANAGER
OFFICE 978-369-1885 MOBILE 978-335-1160 FAX 978-369-1887
LOCATION 37 Main Street Suite #4, Concord, MA 01742
EMAIL janine@ideaplatforms.com WEB www.ideaplatforms.com

IDEA PLATFORMS

The **Butman Company** Inc.

005

HILLTOP
FITNESS

JOSH HILL
OWNER/EXERCISE SPECIALIST
B.S. Exercise Science + B.S. Biology
A.S. Nutrition + NASM-CPT
CSCS Exercise Specialist + ACE-CPT
AHA Level 2 & 3 Cardiac Specialist

josh@hilltopfit.com
T 630 940 5077

Where precision & innovation
create a healthier you
www.hilltopfit.com

EAN ANDREWS
Director
dandrews@hsong.org

210 W. River Drive
St. Charles, IL 60174
P 630.377.0800 F 630.587.9696
www.hsong.org

HARRIETTE'S SONG

A Change of

DAVIDSON
D E S I G N S

SUZY DAVIDSON
INTERIOR I COLOR I FLORAL

suzy@davidson-designs.com

2737 ANDREWS AVE I BATAVIA
630 849 8

davidson

Brian MacDo
brian@macdonaldpho

22WE
GLE

P 630-79
F 630-790-218

macdonaldphotography.com

MacDonald
PHOTOGRAPHY

dvdnow

XING CHEN VP - Engineering
xchen@dvdnowfreemovies.com

659 Executive Drive
Willowbrook, IL 60527
P 630 986 4422
F 630 325 5532

owfreemovies.com

ABOUT THE AUTHOR

R

We believe that
CREATIVE MATTERS.

KEY CHARACTERISTICS

Rule29 is a strategic creative firm that "makes creative matter" by fusing aesthetics with emotion and smart thinking with unique visual messaging. Not only do we design and manage a wide variety of corporate communication services including brand and identity development, social media, package design, advertising, and book design, we also do it in a manner that shows we care for our community and our world. Let's connect. *www.rule29.com*

NOTES

DESIGNER
DIRECTORY

D

{nine}

10 Associates
DESIGN FIRM

6A Cartwright Court
Dyson Wood Way
Huddersfield HD2 1GN, UK
LOCATION

+44.014.84.543905
PHONE

www.10associates.co.uk
WEBSITE

145
SPECIMENS (PAGES)

212-BIG-BOLT
DESIGN FIRM

523 6th Avenue #2
New York, NY 10011
USA
LOCATION

212.244.2658
PHONE

www.bigbolt.com
WEBSITE

193
SPECIMENS (PAGES)

3rd Edge Communications
DESIGN FIRM

162 Newark Avenue
Jersey City, NJ 07302
USA
LOCATION

201.395.9960
PHONE

www.3rdedge.com
WEBSITE

054, 063, 129
SPECIMENS (PAGES)

427 Design
DESIGN FIRM

190 N. Union Street, Suite 200
Akron, OH 44304
USA
LOCATION

330.535.0427
PHONE

www.427design.com
WEBSITE

083
SPECIMENS (PAGES)

A3 Design
DESIGN FIRM

PO Box 43046
Charlotte, NC 28215
USA
LOCATION

704.568.5351
PHONE

www.athreedesign.com
WEBSITE

062, 162
SPECIMENS (PAGES)

Adapter Design
DESIGN FIRM

4421 Yates Street
Denver, CO 80212
USA
LOCATION

720.988.8782
PHONE

www.adapterdesign.com
WEBSITE

209
SPECIMENS (PAGES)

AD Grafica & Comunicazione
DESIGN FIRM

Via Croce Rossa, 8
Padova 35129
Italy
LOCATION

+39.049.8071966
PHONE

www.adcomunicazione.it
WEBSITE

063
SPECIMENS (PAGES)

Adsoka
DESIGN FIRM

1029 Washington Avenue S
Minneapolis, MN 55104
USA
LOCATION

612.279.2390
PHONE

www.adsoka.com
WEBSITE

067, 097, 119
SPECIMENS (PAGES)

AEN
DESIGN FIRM

734 Yishun Avenue 5, #05-416
Singapore 760734
Singapore
LOCATION

+65.9008.3602
PHONE

www.aenui.com
WEBSITE

138
SPECIMENS (PAGES)

AFFINA
DESIGN FIRM

991 Selby Avenue
St. Paul, MN 55104
USA
LOCATION

651.644.2889
PHONE

www.affinadesign.com
WEBSITE

012, 037, 044, 089, 229
SPECIMENS (PAGES)

Afterhours Group
DESIGN FIRM

8185 E. Lowry Boulevard, Suite 103
Denver, CO 80230
USA
LOCATION

303.340.0048
PHONE

www.afterhoursgroup.com
WEBSITE

046, 205
SPECIMENS (PAGES)

airG
DESIGN FIRM

1155 Robson Street, Suite 706
Vancouver, BC V63 1B5
Canada
LOCATION

604.408.2228
PHONE

www.airg.com
WEBSITE

127
SPECIMENS (PAGES)

Airside
DESIGN FIRM

339 Upper Street
Islington
London N1OPB, UK
LOCATION

+44.02073.549912
PHONE

www.airside.co.uk
WEBSITE

128
SPECIMENS (PAGES)

akrok design
DESIGN FIRM

804 S Stoneman Avenue, Apt. 1
Alhambra, CA 91801
USA
LOCATION

310.980.1394
PHONE

www.akrokdesign.com
WEBSITE

209
SPECIMENS (PAGES)

Alphabet Arm Design
DESIGN FIRM

500 Harrison Avenue, 3R
Boston, MA 02118
USA
LOCATION

617.451.9990
PHONE

www.alphabetarm.com
WEBSITE

124, 132, 160, 229
SPECIMENS (PAGES)

And Creative Production
DESIGN FIRM

70 Remsen Street, Suite 9B
Brooklyn, NY 11201
USA
LOCATION

646.201.8514
PHONE

jfreeouf
WEBSITE

226
SPECIMENS (PAGES)

Andrea Gervasoni Visual Communication
DESIGN FIRM

Via San Sebastiano 20
Zogno/Bergamo/24019
Italy
LOCATION

+39. 0345.91.555
PHONE

www.andrea-gervasoni.it
WEBSITE

150
SPECIMENS (PAGES)

Andru Creative
DESIGN FIRM

26 Grenfeu Street
Mount Gravatt East QLD 4122
Australia
LOCATION

+81.7407.137758
PHONE

www.andru.com.au
WEBSITE

059
SPECIMENS (PAGES)

Another Limited Rebellion
DESIGN FIRM

2701 Edgewood Avenue
Richmond, VA 23222
USA
LOCATION

804.321.6677
PHONE

www.alrdesign.com
WEBSITE

077
SPECIMENS (PAGES)

Archrival
DESIGN FIRM

720 O Street, Lot A
Lincoln, NE 68508
USA
LOCATION

402.435.2525
PHONE

www.archrival.com
WEBSITE

036, 080, 181
SPECIMENS (PAGES)

ARK
DESIGN FIRM

Little Trelabe, Brayshop, Callington
Cornwall, PL1 78QL
UK
LOCATION

+44.01566.782591
PHONE

www.arkstudio.co.uk
WEBSITE

088
SPECIMENS (PAGES)

Artista Muvek
DESIGN FIRM

Kiss Janos Altb. 2418
Budapest, Pestmegye, H-1126
Hungary
LOCATION

+36.30.2895046
PHONE

www.artistamuvek.hu
WEBSITE

167
SPECIMENS (PAGES)

Atomic Dust
DESIGN FIRM

317 N. 11th Street, Suite 300
St. Louis, MO 63101
USA
LOCATION

314.241.2866
PHONE

www.atomicdust.com
WEBSITE

130
SPECIMENS (PAGES)

Base Art Co.
DESIGN FIRM

17 Brickel Street, Suite D
Columbus, OH 43215
USA
LOCATION

614.224.4535
PHONE

www.baseartco.com
WEBSITE

102, 105
SPECIMENS (PAGES)

BBM&D Strategic Branding
DESIGN FIRM

3 Lincoln Drive, Suite A
Ventura, CA 93001
USA
LOCATION

805.667.6671
PHONE

www.bbmd-inc.com
WEBSITE

040
SPECIMENS (PAGES)

Biz-R
DESIGN FIRM

35A Fore Street
Totnes, Devon TQ9 5HN
UK
LOCATION

+44 0 1803.868.989
PHONE

www.biz-r.co.uk
WEBSITE

029, 030, 173
SPECIMENS (PAGES)

Boccalatte
DESIGN FIRM

Suite 507, 55 Holt Street, Surry Hills
Sydney, NSW 2010
Australia
LOCATION

+ 61 2.9211.9411
PHONE

www.boccalatte.com
WEBSITE

022, 027, 132
SPECIMENS (PAGES)

Boom Island
DESIGN FIRM

411 Washington Avenue N
Minneapolis, MN 55401
USA
LOCATION

612.343.0042
PHONE

www.boomisland.com
WEBSITE

151
SPECIMENS (PAGES)

Brandhouse
DESIGN FIRM

8A Ledbury Mews North
London W11 2AF
UK
LOCATION

+44 0 207.79857373
PHONE

be@barndhouse.co.uk
WEBSITE

125
SPECIMENS (PAGES)

Brainforest, Inc.
DESIGN FIRM

2211 N. Elston Avenue #301
Chicago, IL 60614
USA
LOCATION

773.395.2500
PHONE

www.brainforest.com
WEBSITE

180, 208
SPECIMENS (PAGES)

Bronson Ma Creative
DESIGN FIRM

17706 Copper Sunset
San Antonio, TX 78232
USA
LOCATION

214.457.5615
PHONE

www.bronsonma.com
WEBSITE

026, 041
SPECIMENS (PAGES)

Bryska212 Design
DESIGN FIRM

612-6400 Coach Hill Road
Calgary, AB T3H 1B8
Canada
LOCATION

403.988.7033
PHONE

www.bryska212.com
WEBSITE

223
SPECIMENS (PAGES)

C3-Creative Consumer Concepts
DESIGN FIRM

10955 Granada Lane
Overland Park, KS 66211
USA
LOCATION

913.327.2241
PHONE

cevans@c3mail.com
WEBSITE

175
SPECIMENS (PAGES)

Carsten Prenger
DESIGN FIRM

Königgrätzersrt. 59
Duisburg 47053
Germany
LOCATION

+49.0777.619.1210
PHONE

carsten.prenger@gmx.net
WEBSITE

011
SPECIMENS (PAGES)

Chen Design Associates
DESIGN FIRM

649 Front Street, 3rd Floor
San Francisco, CA 94111
USA
LOCATION

415.896.5338
PHONE

www.chendesign.com
WEBSITE

049, 108, 158, 214
SPECIMENS (PAGES)

christiansen : creative
DESIGN FIRM

511 2nd Street, Suite 206
Hudson, MN 54016
USA
LOCATION

715.381.8480
PHONE

www.christiansencreative.com
WEBSITE

061, 160
SPECIMENS (PAGES)

Claudia Dionne
DESIGN FIRM

Mazatlan 65-10
Col. Condesa
Mexico 06140, DF
LOCATION

+525.555535364
PHONE

cladila@gmail.com
WEBSITE

129
SPECIMENS (PAGES)

Clayton Junior
DESIGN FIRM

31 Torriano Cotta GES
London NW5 2TA
UK
LOCATION

+44.0 7511.891.644
PHONE

www.claytonjunior.com
WEBSITE

164
SPECIMENS (PAGES)

Clear Space
DESIGN FIRM

159 Main Street, Unit 1
Unionville, ON L3R 2G8
Canada
LOCATION

905.479.9788
PHONE

www.clearspace.ca
WEBSITE

032, 076, 156, 157
SPECIMENS (PAGES)

Clif Bar & Company
DESIGN FIRM

1610 Fifth Street
Berkeley, CA 94710
USA
LOCATION

510.556.7855
PHONE

www.clifbar.com
WEBSITE

071
SPECIMENS (PAGES)

CMD+SHIFT Design
DESIGN FIRM

101 W. Olympic, 315
Seattle, WA 98119
USA
LOCATION

360.440.2946
PHONE

www.cmdshiftdesign.com
WEBSITE

195
SPECIMENS (PAGES)

Cody Haltom
DESIGN FIRM

2401 E. Sixth Street, 6086
Austin, TX 78702
USA
LOCATION

405.625.5751
PHONE

www.codyhaltom.com
WEBSITE

019, 060
SPECIMENS (PAGES)

Counterform
DESIGN FIRM

10934 SW Celeste Lane, Unit 403
Portland, OR 97225
USA
LOCATION

503.747.3765
PHONE

www.counterform.us
WEBSITE

048, 113
SPECIMENS (PAGES)

Creative Insight, LLC
DESIGN FIRM

88 Main Street, Suite 5
New Canaan, CT 06840
USA
LOCATION

203.594.9409
PHONE

www.creative-insight.com
WEBSITE

077
SPECIMENS (PAGES)

The Creative Method
DESIGN FIRM

10 50 Reservoir Street
Surry Hills, NSW 2010
Australia
LOCATION

+6.128231.9977
PHONE

www.thecreativemethod.com
WEBSITE

050, 057, 104, 105, 208, 211
SPECIMENS (PAGES)

Creative Suitcase
DESIGN FIRM

1012 E. 38th ½ Street
Austin, TX 78751
USA
LOCATION

512.326.3667
PHONE

www.creativesuitcase.com
WEBSITE

156
SPECIMENS (PAGES)

D*MNGOOD
DESIGN FIRM

1301 M Street, NW, Suite 1010
Washington, DC 20005
USA
LOCATION

202.683.8975
PHONE

www.dmngood.com
WEBSITE

021, 022,
SPECIMENS (PAGES)

Damion Hickman Design
DESIGN FIRM

1760 Kaiser Avenue
Irvine, CA 92614
USA
LOCATION

949.261.7857
PHONE

www.damionhickman.com
WEBSITE

194
SPECIMENS (PAGES)

Darken Studios
DESIGN FIRM

390 Queens Quay W., Suite 614
Toronto, ON M5V 3A6
Canada
LOCATION

905.616.2444
PHONE

www.darkenstudios.ca
WEBSITE

045
SPECIMENS (PAGES)

David Dayco
DESIGN FIRM

6390 196th Street, #408
Langley, BC V2Y 1J2
Canada
LOCATION

778.240.9059
PHONE

www.daviddayco.ca
WEBSITE

092, 093
SPECIMENS (PAGES)

DEI Creative
DESIGN FIRM

159 Western Avenue West, Suite 450
Seattle, WA 98119
USA
LOCATION

206.281.4004
PHONE

www.deicreative.com
WEBSITE

067
SPECIMENS (PAGES)

Design Circus
DESIGN FIRM

4861 Keller Road
Hamburg, NY 14075
USA
LOCATION

716.982.7248
PHONE

www.design-circus.com
WEBSITE

086
SPECIMENS (PAGES)

designlab, inc
DESIGN FIRM

45 S. Rock Hill Road
St. Louis, MO 63119
USA
LOCATION

314.962.7702
PHONE

www.designlabinc.com
WEBSITE

162
SPECIMENS (PAGES)

The Designworks Group
DESIGN FIRM

PO Box 1773
Sisters, OR 97759
USA
LOCATION

541.549.1096
PHONE

www.thedesignworksgroup.com
WEBSITE

031, 081, 222
SPECIMENS (PAGES)

Di Depux
DESIGN FIRM

18, Meg. Alexandrou str.
Athens-Dafni 172 35
Greece
LOCATION

+30.210.9755850
PHONE

www.depux.com
WEBSITE

039, 041
SPECIMENS (PAGES)

Dreambox Creative
DESIGN FIRM

PO Box 879
Roseville, CA 95678
USA
LOCATION

916.705.0406
PHONE

www.dreamboxcreative.com
WEBSITE

023
SPECIMENS (PAGES)

Element
DESIGN FIRM

3757 N. High Street
Columbus, OH 43214
USA
LOCATION

614.447.0906
PHONE

www.elementville.com
WEBSITE

071
SPECIMENS (PAGES)

Eleven19
DESIGN FIRM

7701 Pacific Street, Suite 220
Omaha, NE 68114
USA
LOCATION

402.707.1119
PHONE

www.eleven19.com
WEBSITE

082
SPECIMENS (PAGES)

Emedia Creative
DESIGN FIRM

91 Watkin Street, Newtown
2042 NSW
Australia
LOCATION

+61.2.9557.3366
PHONE

www.emedia.com.au
WEBSITE

084
SPECIMENS (PAGES)

Evenson Design Group
DESIGN FIRM

4445 Overland Avenue
Culver City, CA 90230
USA
LOCATION

310.204.1995
PHONE

www.evensondesign.com
WEBSITE

061, 065, 115, 161, 173, 217
SPECIMENS (PAGES)

Extra Credit Projects
DESIGN FIRM

560 5th Street NW, Suite 302
Grand Rapids, MI 49504
USA
LOCATION

616.454.2955
PHONE

www.extracreditprojects.com
WEBSITE

070, 153, 159
SPECIMENS (PAGES)

faculty of design
DESIGN FIRM

2143 Abergeldie Drive
Memphis, TN 38119
USA
LOCATION

901.679.5276
PHONE

www.facultyofdesign.com
WEBSITE

183, 202
SPECIMENS (PAGES)

Faust
DESIGN FIRM

360 N. Redale Road
Riverside, IL 60546
USA
LOCATION

708.447.0608
PHONE

www.faustltd.com
WEBSITE

142, 207
SPECIMENS (PAGES)

Firebelly Design
DESIGN FIRM

2701 W. Thomas, 2nd Floor
Chicago, IL 60622
USA
LOCATION

773.489.3200
PHONE

www.firebellydesign.com
WEBSITE

096, 108, 166
SPECIMENS (PAGES)

Flávio Carvalho
DESIGN FIRM

Rua Jesuino Arruda, 657 ap. 25
Itaim Bibi, Sao Paulo SP 04532-082
Brazil
LOCATION

+55.11.3078.44.01 / 8589 8800
PHONE

www.flaviomcarvalho.com/v2
WEBSITE

050
SPECIMENS (PAGES)

Fridge Creative
DESIGN FIRM

59 Charlotte Road
Hoxton, London EC2A3QT
UK
LOCATION

+44.020.7729.8661
PHONE

www.fridgecreative.co.uk
WEBSITE

185
SPECIMENS (PAGES)

FUNNEL: Eric Kass : Utilitarian + Commercial + Fine : Art
DESIGN FIRM

1969 Spruce Drive
Carmel, IN 46033
USA
LOCATION

317.590.5355
PHONE

www.funnel.tv
WEBSITE

043, 101, 102, 122, 128, 144, 147, 197, 200, 228
SPECIMENS (PAGES)

Fusedmedia
DESIGN FIRM

PO Box 2611 Taren Point
Sydney, NSW 2229
Australia
LOCATION

+61.438.421.093
PHONE

www.fusedmedia.com.au
WEBSITE

056, 212
SPECIMENS (PAGES)

G-Man
DESIGN FIRM

Flat 24, Goodhope Mill
Cross Street, Manchester OL6 7SB
UK
LOCATION

+44. 0773.275.2698
PHONE

www.loosecollective.net
WEBSITE

018, 020, 031, 219
SPECIMENS (PAGES)

Garden Variety Designs
DESIGN FIRM

27 Upland Road
Cambridge, MA 02140
USA
LOCATION

617.895.0180
PHONE

wwwl.gardenvarietydesigns.com
WEBSITE

141
SPECIMENS (PAGES)

Geyrhalter Design
DESIGN FIRM

2525 Main Street, #205
Santa Monica, CA 90405
USA
LOCATION

310.392.7615
PHONE

www.geyrhalter.com
WEBSITE

049
SPECIMENS (PAGES)

Glitschka Studios
DESIGN FIRM

1976 Fitzpatrick Avenue SE
Salem, OR 97306
USA
LOCATION

971.223.6143
PHONE

www.glitschka.com
WEBSITE

038, 040, 042
SPECIMENS (PAGES)

Greco Design
DESIGN FIRM

Rio Verde, 150 Sion
Belo Horizonte-MG 30.310-750
Brazil
LOCATION

+55.31.3287.5835
PHONE

www.grecodesign.com.br
WEBSITE

027, 098, 113, 165, 224
SPECIMENS (PAGES)

Grip Design
DESIGN FIRM

1128 N. Ashland
Chicago, IL 60622
USA
LOCATION

312.906.8020
PHONE

www.gripdesign.com
WEBSITE

015, 085, 126, 187, 193, 195, 196, 221
SPECIMENS (PAGES)

The H Agency
DESIGN FIRM

1055 St. Charles Avenue, Suite 300
New Orleans, LA 70130
USA
LOCATION

504.522.6300
PHONE

www.thehagency.com
WEBSITE

064
SPECIMENS (PAGES)

Handcrafted Media
DESIGN FIRM

253 Washington Street
Monument, CO 80132
USA
LOCATION

719.481.8200
PHONE

www.handcraftedmedia.com
WEBSITE

196
SPECIMENS (PAGES)

Heather Mason Design
DESIGN FIRM

2947 N. 85th Street
Milwaukee, WI 53222
USA
LOCATION

414.750.2544
PHONE

www.hmasondesign.com
WEBSITE

094
SPECIMENS (PAGES)

Hill Design Studios
DESIGN FIRM

PO Box 17264
Salem, OR 97305
USA
LOCATION

503.507.1228
PHONE

www.hilldesignstudios.com
WEBSITE

014,
SPECIMENS (PAGES)

HI(NY), LLC
DESIGN FIRM

40 Renwick Street, 8th Floor
New York, NY 10013
USA
LOCATION

917.669.2638
PHONE

www.hinydesign.com
WEBSITE

013, 014, 047, 198
SPECIMENS (PAGES)

Honest Bros.
DESIGN FIRM

1804A South Pearl Street
Denver, CO 80210
USA
LOCATION

303.847.9225
PHONE

www.honestbros.com
WEBSITE

051, 101
SPECIMENS (PAGES)

Hook
DESIGN FIRM

409 King Street
Charleston, SC 29403
USA
LOCATION

843.853.5532
PHONE

www.hookusa.com
WEBSITE

131
SPECIMENS (PAGES)

Iceberg
DESIGN FIRM

142 Rue Du Bac
75007 Paris
France
LOCATION

+33.1.53.63.15.00
PHONE

www.iceberg.fr
WEBSITE

024, 025
SPECIMENS (PAGES)

Imagine
DESIGN FIRM

The Stables, Ducie Street
Manchester M12JN
UK
LOCATION

+44.0161.272.8334
PHONE

www.imagine-cga.co.uk
WEBSITE

024
SPECIMENS (PAGES)

InsaneFacilities
DESIGN FIRM

23 Kwiatowa Street
94238 Lodz
Poland
LOCATION

+48.693772994
PHONE

www.insanefacilities.com
WEBSITE

054
SPECIMENS (PAGES)

Insight Design Communications
DESIGN FIRM

700 South Marcilene Terrace
Wichita, KS 67218
USA
LOCATION

316.262.0085
PHONE

www.insightdesign.com
WEBSITE

124
SPECIMENS (PAGES)

Intrinsic Design
DESIGN FIRM

1201 N. Creek Court
Alpharetta, GA
USA 30009
LOCATION

770.410.1626
PHONE

www.intrinsic-design.biz
WEBSITE

139
SPECIMENS (PAGES)

janmichael-b
DESIGN FIRM

6126 Compton Street, #7
Indianapolis, IN 46220
USA
LOCATION

317.460.6063
PHONE

www.janmichael-b.com
WEBSITE

226
SPECIMENS (PAGES)

John Fern
DESIGN FIRM

512 S. Cedarcrest Drive
Schaumburg, IL 60193
USA
LOCATION

847.609.4742
PHONE

www.johnferndesign.com
WEBSITE

199
SPECIMENS (PAGES)

Joy Renee Design
DESIGN FIRM

1825 Kendall Street, #201
Denver, CO 80214
USA
LOCATION

952.200.0794
PHONE

www.joyrenee.com
WEBSITE

084
SPECIMENS (PAGES)

Juicebox Designs
DESIGN FIRM

4709 Idaho Avenue
Nashville, TN 37209
USA
LOCATION

615.297.1682
PHONE

www.juiceboxdesigns.com
WEBSITE

227
SPECIMENS (PAGES)

Kelly Boyle Designs
DESIGN FIRM

165 Pearl Street, #36C
Seymour, CT 06483
USA
LOCATION

203.558.1660
PHONE

www.kboyle.com
WEBSITE

089
SPECIMENS (PAGES)

Lefty Lexington Design
DESIGN FIRM

102 Ashberry Lane
Stoughton, WI 53589
USA
LOCATION

608.225.9892
PHONE

www.leftylexington.com
WEBSITE

107
SPECIMENS (PAGES)

Lloyds Graphic Design Ltd.
DESIGN FIRM

17 Westhaven Place
Blenheim
New Zealand
LOCATION

+64.3.578.6955
PHONE

lloydgraphics@xtra.co.uk
WEBSITE

042, 045, 144
SPECIMENS (PAGES)

Louviere + Vanessa
DESIGN FIRM

732 Mazant Street
New Orleans, LA 70117
USA
LOCATION

504.296.5467
PHONE

www.louviereandvanessa.com
WEBSITE

017, 030, 051, 082, 090
SPECIMENS (PAGES)

Maas Design
DESIGN FIRM

2706 Tyler
Berkeley, MI 48072
USA
LOCATION

248.840.7537
PHONE

www.maasdesign.com
WEBSITE

091, 179, 197
SPECIMENS (PAGES)

Marc O'Brien
DESIGN FIRM

744 Dwyer Road
Virginia Beach, VA 23454
USA
LOCATION

804.677.7655
PHONE

www.marcobrien.net
WEBSITE

023
SPECIMENS (PAGES)

MDG DESIGN FIRM	**Modelhart Design** DESIGN FIRM	**Object 9** DESIGN FIRM	**Pascale Payant Design** DESIGN FIRM
13 Water Street, 3rd Floor Holliston, MA 01746 USA LOCATION	Ing.-Ludwig-Pech_Str. 1 St. Johann im Pongau Salzburg 5600, Austria LOCATION	4156 W. E. Heck Court Baton Rouge, LA 70816 USA LOCATION	185 Rue de la Riviére Gatineau, QC J9H 6Z4 Canada LOCATION
508.429.0755 PHONE	+43.6412.4679.0 PHONE	225.368.9899 PHONE	819.790.9277 PHONE
www.thinkmdg.com WEBSITE	www.modelhart.at WEBSITE	www.object9.com WEBSITE	www.p2design.biz WEBSITE
155 SPECIMENS (PAGES)	107 SPECIMENS (PAGES)	152 SPECIMENS (PAGES)	148 SPECIMENS (PAGES)
Megan Cummins DESIGN FIRM	**MSDS** DESIGN FIRM	**Organic Grid** DESIGN FIRM	**Pavone** DESIGN FIRM
698 Bush Street, #503 San Francisco, CA 94108 USA LOCATION	611 Broadway, Suite 430 New York, NY 10012 USA LOCATION	827 Fitzwater Street Philadelphia, PA 19147 USA LOCATION	1006 Market Street Harrisburg, PA 17101 USA LOCATION
415.279.0051 PHONE	212.925.6460 PHONE	215.840.0626 PHONE	717.234.8886 PHONE
www.megancummins.com WEBSITE	www.ms-ds.com WEBSITE	www.organicgrid.com WEBSITE	www.pavone.net WEBSITE
086, 170 SPECIMENS (PAGES)	010, 016, 190, 193 SPECIMENS (PAGES)	171 SPECIMENS (PAGES)	109, 110 SPECIMENS (PAGES)
Miller + Miller DESIGN FIRM	**Murillo Design, Inc.** DESIGN FIRM	**Ours Creative** DESIGN FIRM	**People Design** DESIGN FIRM
409 Cascade Lane Oswego, IL 60543 USA LOCATION	816 Camaron, Studio 216 San Antonio, TX 28212 USA LOCATION	390 Queens Quay W., Suite 614 Toronto, ON M5V 3A6 Cananda LOCATION	648 Monroe NW, Suite 212 Grand Rapids, MI 49503 USA LOCATION
630.373.2411 PHONE	210.248.9412 PHONE	905.616.2444 PHONE	616.459.4444 PHONE
www.millermillerllc.com WEBSITE	www.murillodesign.com WEBSITE	www.ourscreative.com WEBSITE	www.peopledesign.com WEBSITE
181, 184 SPECIMENS (PAGES)	225 SPECIMENS (PAGES)	017 SPECIMENS (PAGES)	010 SPECIMENS (PAGES)
MINE DESIGN FIRM	**Neoscape** DESIGN FIRM	**Oxide Design Co.** DESIGN FIRM	**Ph.D, A Design Office** DESIGN FIRM
190 Putnam Street San Francisco, CA 94110 USA LOCATION	330 Congress Street Boston, MA 02210 USA LOCATION	3916 Farnam Street Omaha, NE 68131 USA LOCATION	1524A Cloverfield Boulevard Santa Monica, CA 90404 USA LOCATION
415.647.6463 PHONE	617.345.0330 PHONE	402.344.0168 PHONE	310.829.0900 PHONE
www.minesf.com WEBSITE	www.neoscape.com WEBSITE	www.oxidedesign.com WEBSITE	www.phdla.com WEBSITE
025, 152, 229 SPECIMENS (PAGES)	216 SPECIMENS (PAGES)	075, 165, 209 SPECIMENS (PAGES)	227 SPECIMENS (PAGES)
Miriello Grafico DESIGN FIRM	**Netra Nei** DESIGN FIRM	**P22 Type Foundry** DESIGN FIRM	**Pink Blue Black & Orange Co., Ltd.** DESIGN FIRM
1660 Logan Avenue San Diego, CA 92113 USA LOCATION	845 Bellevue Place E #108 Seattle, WA 98102 USA LOCATION	WNY Book Arts Center PO Box 770 Buffalo, NY 14213 USA LOCATION	428 Rama 9 Road, Guanluang Bangkok 10250 Thailand LOCATION
619.234.1124 PHONE	206.240.3582 PHONE	716.903.6875 PHONE	+ 66.2.300.5124 PHONE
www.miriellografico.com WEBSITE	www.netranei.com WEBSITE	www.wnybookarts.org WEBSITE	www.pbbando.com WEBSITE
158 SPECIMENS (PAGES)	210 SPECIMENS (PAGES)	039 SPECIMENS (PAGES)	060, 116 SPECIMENS (PAGES)
Mirko Ilić Corp. DESIGN FIRM	**Ó!** DESIGN FIRM	**Paper Tower** DESIGN FIRM	**Plazma Design** DESIGN FIRM
207 E. 32nd Street New York, NY 10016 USA LOCATION	Armuli 1 Reykjavik 108 Iceland LOCATION	626 Congdon Avenue Elgin, IL 60120 USA LOCATION	8 Upper Lancaster Road, Ascot Brisbane, Queensland 4007 Australia LOCATION
212.481.9737 PHONE	+35. 562.3300 PHONE	847.513.2063 PHONE	+61.7.3862.6025 PHONE
www.mirkoilic.com WEBSITE	www.oid.is WEBSITE	www.papertower.com WEBSITE	hansson6@gmail.com WEBSITE
048, 106, 186, 210, 228 SPECIMENS (PAGES)	139 SPECIMENS (PAGES)	222 SPECIMENS (PAGES)	070, 072, 073, 215, 217 SPECIMENS (PAGES)

Prescott Perez-Fox
DESIGN FIRM

219 First Street, 4th Floor
Jersey City, NJ 07302
USA
LOCATION

973.900.1588
PHONE

www.perezfox.com
WEBSITE

112
SPECIMENS (PAGES)

Prime Studio
DESIGN FIRM

315 W. 39th Street, Suite 1101
New York, NY 10018
USA
LOCATION

212.239.2395
PHONE

www.primestudio.com
WEBSITE

205
SPECIMENS (PAGES)

Range
DESIGN FIRM

2257 Vantage Street
Dallas, TX 75207
USA
LOCATION

214.744.0555
PHONE

www.rangeus.com
WEBSITE

056
SPECIMENS (PAGES)

RDQLUS Creative
DESIGN FIRM

7701 Pierce Street, #4
Omaha, NE 68124
USA
LOCATION

402.212.0108
PHONE

www.rdqlus.com
WEBSITE

068
SPECIMENS (PAGES)

Reactor
DESIGN FIRM

3111 Wyandotte, Suite 203
Kansas City, MO 64111
USA
LOCATION

816.841.3682
PHONE

www.yourreactor.com
WEBSITE

021, 169
SPECIMENS (PAGES)

Real Art Design Group
DESIGN FIRM

232 E. Sixth Street
Dayton, OH 45402
USA
LOCATION

937.223.9955
PHONE

www.realartusa.com
WEBSITE

011, 012, 111, 202, 207
SPECIMENS (PAGES)

Rehybrid
DESIGN FIRM

Blk 644 #05-26
Woodlands Ring Road
Singapore 730644
LOCATION

+65.9435.5830
PHONE

www.rehybrid.com
WEBSITE

052
SPECIMENS (PAGES)

Robert Meyers Design
DESIGN FIRM

301 Grant Street, Suite 825
Pittsburgh, PA 15219
USA
LOCATION

412.288.9933
PHONE

www.robertmeyersdesign.com
WEBSITE

149
SPECIMENS (PAGES)

Robin Easter Design
DESIGN FIRM

132 W. Jackson Avenue
Knoxville, TN 37902
USA
LOCATION

865.524.0146
PHONE

www.robineaster.com
WEBSITE

114, 117, 119, 126, 133, 220
SPECIMENS (PAGES)

Royal Fly LLP
DESIGN FIRM

442 Serangoon Road, Level 4
Singapore 218135

LOCATION

+65.6293.3962
PHONE

www.royal-fly.com
WEBSITE

154, 191
SPECIMENS (PAGES)

Roycroft Design
DESIGN FIRM

7 Faneuil Hall Marketplace, 4th Floor
Boston, MA 02109
USA
LOCATION

617.720.4506
PHONE

www.roycroftdesign.com
WEBSITE

085
SPECIMENS (PAGES)

Rule29 Creative
DESIGN FIRM

501 Hamilton Street
Geneva, IL 60134
USA
LOCATION

630.262.1009
PHONE

www.rule29.com
WEBSITE

066, 072, 075, 120, 121, 191
SPECIMENS (PAGES)

Rutka Weadock Design
DESIGN FIRM

1627 E. Baltimore Street
Baltimore, MD 21231
USA
LOCATION

410.563.2100
PHONE

www.rutkaweadock.com
WEBSITE

018, 150, 213, 224
SPECIMENS (PAGES)

Sabine Zimmerman
DESIGN FIRM

Cranger Str. 15a
44625 Herne
Germany
LOCATION

+43.023231.959528
PHONE

bine.zim@web.de
WEBSITE

104
SPECIMENS (PAGES)

Selena Chen
DESIGN FIRM

40 Avenue D, Apt. 13C
New York, NY 10009
USA
LOCATION

646.421.8284
PHONE

scrabbit@gmail.com
WEBSITE

180, 197
SPECIMENS (PAGES)

Sophy (Sorim) Lee
DESIGN FIRM

School of Visual Arts, MFA
808 West End Avenue, #707
New York, NY 10025
LOCATION

917.613.3598
PHONE

www.sophylee.com
WEBSITE

106, 137, 199
SPECIMENS (PAGES)

Scott Adams Design Associates
DESIGN FIRM

290 Market Street, Suite 803
Minneapolis, MN 55405
USA
LOCATION

612.236.1146
PHONE

www.sadesigna.com
WEBSITE

154
SPECIMENS (PAGES)

Peter Sexty Design
DESIGN FIRM

Aria Building, Suite 305
CNR Surf PDE & Albert Ave Broadbeach
Queensland 4218, Australia
LOCATION

+07.5539.9399
PHONE

www.sextydesign.com.au/
WEBSITE

216
SPECIMENS (PAGES)

Shelby Designs & Illustrates
DESIGN FIRM

155 Filbert Street, Suite 216
Oakland, CA 94607
USA
LOCATION

510.444.0502
PHONE

www.shelbydesigns.com
WEBSITE

065, 218
SPECIMENS (PAGES)

Siquis
DESIGN FIRM

1340 Smith Avenue, Suite 300
Baltimore, MD 21209
USA
LOCATION

410.323.4800
PHONE

www.siquis.com
WEBSITE

036
SPECIMENS (PAGES)

Socio Design
DESIGN FIRM

24 Greville Street
London EC1N 8SS
UK
LOCATION

+44.0.20.3008.4443
PHONE

www.sociodesign.co.uk
WEBSITE

120
SPECIMENS (PAGES)

sparc, inc.
DESIGN FIRM

824 Humboldt Avenue
Winnetka, IL 60093
USA
LOCATION

847.784.3100
PHONE

www.sparcinc.com
WEBSITE

052
SPECIMENS (PAGES)

Spark! Communications
DESIGN FIRM

327 E. Maryland
Royal Oak, MI 48067
USA
LOCATION

248.545.9012
PHONE

www.spark-communications.com
WEBSITE

053, 161
SPECIMENS (PAGES)

Spring
DESIGN FIRM

1250 Homer Street, 301
Vancouver, BC V6B 1C6
Canada
LOCATION

604.683.0167 x 321
PHONE

www.springadvertising.com
WEBSITE

073, 166, 168, 218
SPECIMENS (PAGES)

Square Feet Design
DESIGN FIRM

11 Park Place, Suite 1705
New York, NY 10007
USA
LOCATION

646.237.2828
PHONE

www.squarefeetdesign.com
WEBSITE

096, 204
SPECIMENS (PAGES)

squarehand.com
DESIGN FIRM

21-38 31st Street, #5P
Astoria, NY 11105
USA
LOCATION

646.285.5600
PHONE

www.squarehand.com
WEBSITE

055, 147, 154
SPECIMENS (PAGES)

St. Bernadine Mission Communications, Inc.
DESIGN FIRM

#802-318 Homer Street
Vancouver, BC V6B 2V2
Canada
LOCATION

604.646.0001
PHONE

www.stbernadine.com
WEBSITE

162
SPECIMENS (PAGES)

Steve Scott Graphic Design
DESIGN FIRM

6/12-20 Rosebank Street
Darlinghurst NSW 2010
Australia
LOCATION

+61.424.386.715
PHONE

www.stevescottgraphicdesign.com
WEBSITE

016, 019, 117
SPECIMENS (PAGES)

Stressdesign
DESIGN FIRM

1001 W. Fayette Street, Floor 1
Syracuse, NY 13204
USA
LOCATION

315.422.3231 x 204
PHONE

www.stressdesign.com
WEBSITE

172
SPECIMENS (PAGES)

Struck
DESIGN FIRM

159 W. Broadway, Suite 200
Salt Lake City, UT 84101
USA
LOCATION

801.531.0122
PHONE

www.struckcreative.com
WEBSITE

210, 167, 214
SPECIMENS (PAGES)

Studio Conover
DESIGN FIRM

800 W. Ivy Street, Studio C
San Diego, CA 92101
USA
LOCATION

619.238.1999 x105
PHONE

www.studioconover.com
WEBSITE

068, 115, 183
SPECIMENS (PAGES)

Studio Tigrafik
DESIGN FIRM

E. Pynaertraai 115/20 1
9000 Ghent
Belgium
LOCATION

+32.0.479.35.33.82
PHONE

www.tigrafik.com
WEBSITE

213
SPECIMENS (PAGES)

studiovertex
DESIGN FIRM

108 S. Washington Street, Suite 310
Seattle, WA 98104
USA
LOCATION

206.838.7240
PHONE

www.studio-vertex.com
WEBSITE

103, 182
SPECIMENS (PAGES)

Stun Design & Advertising
DESIGN FIRM

442 Government Street
Baton Rouge, LA 70802
USA
LOCATION

225.381.7266
PHONE

www.stundesign.net
WEBSITE

111
SPECIMENS (PAGES)

tasteofinkstudios.com
DESIGN FIRM

7001 E. Main Street
Scottsdale, AZ 85251
USA
LOCATION

877.988.2783
PHONE

www.tasteofinkstudios.com
WEBSITE

081, 133, 202
SPECIMENS (PAGES)

Ten26 Design Group, Inc.
DESIGN FIRM

432 Diamondo Street
Crystal Lake, IL 60012
USA
LOCATION

847.650.3282
PHONE

www.ten26design.com
WEBSITE

062, 091, 206
SPECIMENS (PAGES)

Third Sector Creative
DESIGN FIRM

338 N. Milwaukee Street, Suite 207
Milwaukee, WI 53202
USA
LOCATION

414.302.0200
PHONE

www.thirdsectorcreative.com
WEBSITE

137
SPECIMENS (PAGES)

Timber Design Company Inc.
DESIGN FIRM

4402 N. College Avenue
Indianapolis, IN 46205
USA
LOCATION

317.213.8509
PHONE

www.timberdesignco.com
WEBSITE

046, 055, 100, 149
SPECIMENS (PAGES)

tmarks design
DESIGN FIRM

803 S. King Street
Seattle, WA 98104
USA
LOCATION

206.628.6427
PHONE

www.tmarksdesign.com
WEBSITE

037, 044, 136, 140
SPECIMENS (PAGES)

TOKY Branding + Design
DESIGN FIRM

3001 Locust Street, 2nd Floor
St. Louis, MO 63103
USA
LOCATION

314.534.2000
PHONE

www.toky.com
WEBSITE

032, 092, 094, 095, 097, 099, 112, 121, 131, 143,
179, 185, 200, 201, 203
SPECIMENS (PAGES)

Tomato Kosir S.P.
DESIGN FIRM

Britof 141
51-4000, Kranj
Slovenia, EU
LOCATION

+386.0 41.260.979
PHONE

www.behance.net/tomato
WEBSITE

123
SPECIMENS (PAGES)

Tomko Design
DESIGN FIRM

6868 N. 7th Avenue, Suite 210
Phoenix, AZ 85013
USA
LOCATION

602.412.4002
PHONE

www.tomkodesign.com
WEBSITE

026, 028, 116, 187, 192, 206
SPECIMENS (PAGES)

---

traciedesigns
DESIGN FIRM

693 Jennings Road
Fairfield, CT 06824
USA
LOCATION

203.243.8175
PHONE

www.traciedesigns.net
WEBSITE

028, 182
SPECIMENS (PAGES)

Travis Blake
DESIGN FIRM

16 Winthrop Street
West Boylston, MA 01583
USA
LOCATION

617.935.1705
PHONE

www.travisblake.com
WEBSITE

221
SPECIMENS (PAGES)

Two Twenty Two Creative
DESIGN FIRM

17055 Mt. Lyndora
Fountain Valley, CA 92708
USA
LOCATION

949.836.7316
PHONE

www.222creative.com
WEBSITE

118
SPECIMENS (PAGES)

Type G
DESIGN FIRM

143 S. Cedros Avenue, Suite B205
Solana Beach, CA 92075
USA
LOCATION

858.792.7333
PHONE

www.launchtypeg.com
WEBSITE

069, 168
SPECIMENS (PAGES)

Unfold Studio
DESIGN FIRM

7 Chy Cober, Hayle
Cornwall TR27 4PA
UK
LOCATION

+44 0 7929802892
PHONE

www.unfoldstudio.com
WEBSITE

033
SPECIMENS (PAGES)

visure
DESIGN FIRM

31 Kingfisher Lane
East Brisbane
Queensland 4169, Australia
LOCATION

+61 7.3391.2547
PHONE

www.visure.com.au
WEBSITE

159
SPECIMENS (PAGES)

Voicebox Creative
DESIGN FIRM

3 Meacham Place
San Francisco, CA 94109
USA
LOCATION

415.674.3200
PHONE

www.voiceboxcreative.com
WEBSITE

058, 118, 163
SPECIMENS (PAGES)

Waterform Design Inc.
DESIGN FIRM

30 Waterside Plaza
New York, NY 10010
USA
LOCATION

212.684.5012
PHONE

www.masayonai.com
WEBSITE

180
SPECIMENS (PAGES)

Paige Weber
DESIGN FIRM

1811 Division Avenue
Boise, ID 83706
USA
LOCATION

208.484.0499
PHONE

www.pgweber.com
WEBSITE

145
SPECIMENS (PAGES)

Wendy Polish
DESIGN FIRM

1428 Graynold Avenue
Glendale, CA 91202
USA
LOCATION

323.788.8707
PHONE

www.wendypolish.com
WEBSITE

212
SPECIMENS (PAGES)

Westwerk Design
DESIGN FIRM

126 N. 3rd Street, #305
Minneapolis, MN 55401
USA
LOCATION

612.251.4277
PHONE

www.westwerkdesign.com
WEBSITE

074, 114, 164, 219
SPECIMENS (PAGES)

white_space
DESIGN FIRM

6677 Delmar Boulevard
St. Louis, MO 63130
USA
LOCATION

314.255.9531
PHONE

www.findthewhitespace.com
WEBSITE

170
SPECIMENS (PAGES)

Wicked Creative
DESIGN FIRM

6120 Tropicana Avenue, Suite A-16, #152
Las Vegas, NV 89103
USA
LOCATION

702.325.0380
PHONE

gabesmail@cox.net
WEBSITE

043
SPECIMENS (PAGES)

Willoughby Design
DESIGN FIRM

602 Westport Road
Kansas City, MO 64111
USA
LOCATION

816.561.4189
PHONE

www.willoughbydesign.com
WEBSITE

153, 224
SPECIMENS (PAGES)

With Creative
DESIGN FIRM

243 Fifth Avenue, Suite 434
New York, NY 10016
USA
LOCATION

917.208.0297
PHONE

www.withcreative.com
WEBSITE

173
SPECIMENS (PAGES)

WORKtoDATE
DESIGN FIRM

York, PA 17403
USA

LOCATION

717.683.5712
PHONE

www.worktodate.com
WEBSITE

083
SPECIMENS (PAGES)

wp2 design
DESIGN FIRM

2225 Abergeldie Drive
Memphis, TN 38119
USA
LOCATION

901.277.7911
PHONE

www.wp2design.com
WEBSITE

058
SPECIMENS (PAGES)

Z2 Marketing
DESIGN FIRM

W237 N2889 Woodgate Road
Unit Z
Pewaukee, WI 53072
LOCATION

262.523.3900
PHONE

www.z2marketing.com
WEBSITE

146
SPECIMENS (PAGES)

Zande + Newman Design
DESIGN FIRM

902 Jefferson Avenue, No. 1
New Orleans, LA 70125
USA
LOCATION

504.891.4526
PHONE

www.zandenewman.com
WEBSITE

146, 149, 190
SPECIMENS (PAGES)

Zync Communications
DESIGN FIRM

282 Richmond Street East, Suite 200
Toronto, ON M5A 1P4
Canada
LOCATION

416.322.2865 x234
PHONE

www.zync.ca
WEBSITE

087, 223
SPECIMENS (PAGES)